Praise for
Managing Concentrated Stock Wealth
by Tim Kochis

"**Finally someone has prepared the comprehensive guide for handling concentrated stock positions.** Tim Kochis has long been a leader in the advisory community and built his business at ground zero of the technology stock market boom. He and his partners were forced to develop an unmatched expertise in helping clients manage large, single-stock positions resulting from their employment. In this book, he shares his vast experience and insights with other advisers."

MARK HURLEY
CEO, Undiscovered Managers

"Anyone who works with clients with inherited wealth or with corporate executives should keep this book prominently displayed on his desk. **I have been referring to it more frequently than the yellow pages!**"

ROSS LEVIN, CFP
President, Accredited Investors, Inc.
Author, *The Wealth Management Index*

"**If you can't get Tim Kochis to advise you on your concentrated positions, buy this book for your adviser.**"

RICHARD A. KASHNOW, PHD
Former Chairman and CEO, Raychem
Non-Executive Chairman, Komag

"For those financial planners and investment advisers who work even occasionally with clients who have concentrated stock positions, *Managing Concentrated Stock Wealth* will be a time-saver. **Tim Kochis has shared his extensive experience and knowledge with us by thoughtfully addressing all the strategies—from simple to complex.** With this resource available, we have more time to focus on matching our clients' goals with the appropriate strategies."

ELAINE E. BEDEL, CFP
President, Bedel Financial Consulting, Inc.

"Tim Kochis has another hit with his latest book, *Managing Concentrated Stock Wealth*. Advisers working with highly compensated executives will find this book to be **an invaluable resource** as they deal with the complex issues surrounding concentrated stock positions."

TOM L. POTTS, PHD, CFP
Professor of Finance and FSP Program Director
Baylor University Hankamer School of Business

"Tim Kochis's book is unique in offering comprehensive, one-stop consideration of this common client problem. **It should be in every planner's library.**"

JERRY J. MCCOY
Attorney, Law Office of Jerry J. McCoy

"Tim Kochis is the planner's planner, and *Managing Concentrated Stock Wealth* is **essential reading for any adviser helping clients navigate the return, risk, tax, legal, charitable, and psychological issues that come with concentrated wealth**. An indispensable book."

PAUL SOLLI
Partner, Aperio Group LLC

"**If you have even one client with a concentrated stock position, this is a must-read.** Kochis combines decades of experience, exceptional technical knowledge, and a gift for writing to create an invaluable guide to this thorny issue."

HAROLD EVENSKY
Chairman, Evensky & Katz

"**No one knows this subject as well as Tim Kochis.** This book is the 'bible' for all of us who work with clients whose wealth is concentrated in a single stock."

PEGGY M. RUHLIN, CFP, CPA/PFS
Principal, Budros, Ruhlin & Roe, Inc.

Managing Concentrated Stock Wealth

Managing Concentrated Stock Wealth

An Adviser's Guide to Building Customized Solutions

Tim Kochis

BLOOMBERG PRESS
NEW YORK

First edition published 2005
1 3 5 7 9 10 8 6 4 2

Library of Congress Cataloging-in-Publication Data

Kochis, Tim
Managing concentrated stock wealth : an adviser's guide to building customized solutions / by Tim Kochis. -- 1st ed.
p. cm.
Summary: "Explains to financial advisers a wide range of strategies for managing concentrated stock positions, including sale, gifts to charity and family, and retention"--Provided by publisher.
Includes index.
ISBN 1-57660-177-3 (alk. paper)
1. Portfolio management. 2. Stocks. 3. Investments. 4. Finance, Personal. I. Title.

HG4529.5.K63 2005
332.63' 22—dc22

2005005680

Acquired by Jared Kieling

Edited by Mary Ann McGuigan

For my father, Stephen Kochis, and my father-in-law, Henry Wong.
Neither of them ever had significant financial resources,
but both enjoyed a great wealth of practical wisdom,
the guiding principle of this book.

Contents

Foreword

CONCENTRATED STOCK POSITIONS are among the most familiar issues financial advisers face—and one of the oldest. They long predate the tech boom that eventually unbalanced so many portfolios in the late 1990s, and they're likely to remain part of the job of managing wealth as long as stock and options are part of executive compensation. Virtually every book on investing describes the risks of concentrated wealth and identifies at least a few techniques for dealing with it—as a problem. Very few treat concentration as a potential opportunity.

It's fair to say that almost every investor is aware of concentration as an important investment issue and that every financial adviser recognizes the need to be able to respond to the concerns investors have about it. In January 2004, *Registered Rep* magazine presented a survey of nearly 400 senior executives holding concentrated stock positions and more than 600 advisers. It attempted to measure how concerned the executives were, as well as how aware advisers were of the options for addressing the problem. Nearly 72 percent of the executive sample reported being "worried" about their lack of diversification. The adviser group as a whole was "not aware of all the options available."

It would certainly be better for their clients if they were. *Managing Concentrated Stock Wealth: An Adviser's Guide to Building Customized Solutions* is designed to put in one place a thorough review of the many techniques advisers have available to manage their clients' concentrated stock wealth—both to reduce risk and to maximize opportunity. The book is an attempt to set out more than thirty years' experience with thousands of clients, most of whom have had some form of stock holding that others, at least, would call concentrated. Some of these clients hadn't recognized any special issues associated with their stock holdings; they were neither aware of any particular risks nor eager for any particular excess returns. Others, however, were quick to dismiss any concerns about such risk as naive, uninformed, or unworthy of the entrepreneurial spirit they wanted to cultivate in themselves or others. Most, however, were very happy to have a guide through the often-confusing maze of managing this aspect of their wealth. Here, then, is what I've learned about how to educate clients on the risks and opportunities related to concentrated stock positions and how best to manage these assets to achieve their objectives.

The book is organized so that the most straightforward solutions are introduced first, followed sequentially by others, each increasingly complex. That path has two purposes. First, it allows us to more thoroughly address the cumulative nature of the more complex strategies. Deploying a costless collar, for example, presumes a considerable degree of understanding of the more fundamental techniques. The second purpose is to lay out a pattern of choices to consider for the client. If the client's problem can be solved with one of the simpler approaches, there may be no reason to go further. This triage is valuable even if you expect that the optimal strategy for a particular client situation is far along the scale of complexity. Clients often surprise us. Once exposed to a *simple* course of action, they often abandon what we thought was their taste for something more elaborate, and once exposed to the costs and risks of those more elaborate strategies, they often want to go back to something more tame.

The chapters that follow are grouped broadly into three areas—one dealing with various approaches to the *disposition* of the stock by selling (or not buying), the second dealing with gifts to family and to charity, and the third dealing with managing *retention* of the holding. As will become clear, no approach needs to be deployed in isolation. Very often, in fact, several of them can be combined to meet the idiosyncrasies of a particular client's range of needs and desires.

Although financial advisers are the primary audience for this book, clients should find it valuable as well. They'll identify with the many examples I've drawn from actual clients to illustrate the concepts presented. They'll be comforted to know that they aren't the first or the only ones to face the particularly thorny financial situations that concentrated stock can create—especially if the eventual outcome on display is good. Perhaps even more important, clients can develop much greater confidence that objective, experienced help is available. Their advisers truly are in a position to help and have many effective tools at the ready.

Acknowledgments

I have many people to thank for their help in making this book possible. Let me begin with my wife, Penelope Wong, herself a writer, for her inspiration and for her patience with me over the many evenings and weekends devoted to this work. My Kochis Fitz colleagues come close behind for encouraging my efforts.

Special thanks go to my executive assistant of many years, Marilyn Drobenaire, for handling what seemed to me thousands of details as this project unfolded; to Ken Wu for his work on the many drafts of the text; and to my research assistant, Victoria Wong, for nearly overwhelming me with helpful material.

While I take responsibility for any flaws that might remain, I am deeply indebted to Tom Potts, PhD, Richard Kinyon, Esq., and Myron Sugarman, Esq., for their careful reading of early versions of the text and for their many worthwhile suggestions, and to the editorial staff at Bloomberg Press for their guidance and discipline along the way in bringing this book to completion.

But I owe my greatest debt of gratitude to the many clients with concentrated stock positions, who have given me the opportunity, over many years, to learn how best to help them achieve their financial goals. This book is about them and for the benefit of others like them.

Introduction

HOLDING A CONCENTRATED stock position is unwise, at least theoretically, because of the downside risk. Mainstream investment theory holds that one is not compensated for taking risks that can be reduced.[1] Since diversification of a concentrated position would mitigate its risk, failing to diversify means one is accepting risk for no *expected* reward—well, at least not expected by other investors in the marketplace.

Most people, of course, are eager to maximize their risk-adjusted investment returns. But some can't easily do so because of concerns over tax liability on holdings with large capital gains. Particularly for corporate executives, the alternatives for addressing the problem are often constrained by post–initial public offering "lockups," specific employer-mandated shareholding requirements, and Securities and Exchange Commission restrictions on short-term trading or on the use of inside information. Such limitations notwithstanding, many techniques are available—some very simple, others quite elaborate—for easing this concentration risk.

Getting the Priorities Straight

Early in 2002, I met with prospective clients, a couple in their late 50s. The husband had just retired from a long and successful career with a large public company. Their largest individual holding was more than $8 million in his employer's stock. Its price had been falling, and the couple was quite agitated about what to do to preserve this large value. They had already consulted other advisers and were confused. "Some people say we should do puts or buy a collar. One adviser told us to do something called a 'prepaid forward.' Frankly, I don't understand that. I hope you can help."

"All of those things, and others, could be appropriate," I explained, "but let's start with the simplest steps. We could just sell it. Even if your basis were zero, the worst that would happen is you incur federal capital-gains tax of 20 percent." (This was before the 2003 tax law changed the federal capital-gains rate to 15 percent.) "With the remaining 80 percent, you get to do whatever you want," I said. "Things get better if you have any basis at all."

"We don't have any net gains in this holding," the husband shot back. "Overall, it's at a loss."

"Well, then, why don't we just sell it—today?" At that suggestion, his wife jumped up, came around the conference table, and planted a big kiss on my cheek—and I had a new client.

The advice this couple had been offered as they shopped for an adviser demonstrates that too frequently advisers are so in love with fancy strategies that they neglect to inquire about the most basic facts of a client's circumstances—such as the tax basis—and fail to gauge the client's appetite for complex solutions. The simplest fixes are often the best in terms of controlling costs, reducing delay, and gaining clients' confidence in the outcome.

It is crucial to recognize that a client's appetite for complexity or for structural risks (will the counterparty to a put be solvent when the put is executed?) or for tax-compliance risks (will exchange funds continue to qualify for tax deferral?) is not necessarily the same as the adviser's. Some clients are inclined to be very aggressive, in eager pursuit of elaborate techniques. In our experience, however, these people are the exceptions. Most clients are a lot less knowledgeable and, consequently, a good deal less comfortable with sophisticated strategy alternatives than their advisers are.

Moreover, their respective motivations can be very different. Every adviser has had the experience of attending a professional conference, hearing a presentation on a new strategy or a new enhancement to an old approach, and recognizing that he's not up to speed on it. One of the presenter's goals, of course, is to engender fear and guilt in his audience for their lack of complete mastery of every new, sophisticated technique. This is one of the ways a profession advances its art. Advisers are eager to achieve—and demonstrate—that mastery, motivated by the desire to maintain or advance their standing among their peers. But that's not what motivates the client. And a demonstration of the adviser's virtuosity in a particular strategy doesn't help much if it isn't, in fact, the best solution for the client. Often the best approach is one that's simple, fast, low cost, and with little regulatory or tax exposure. Occam's razor—first implemented in medieval philosophy and avidly adopted by the physical sciences—applies here as well: the simplest answer is probably correct.

Knowing the Client

As in all aspects of financial planning, the only legitimate starting place for dealing with a concentrated stock position is an understanding of the client's objectives. Does the client want to accomplish a business goal (acquire or maintain control of an enterprise, for example) that necessitates some degree of concentration? Or does the client want to support an expense target that requires a reasonably predictable cash flow stream that would be jeopardized by the risks of concentration?

Advisers must be sensitive to clients' idiosyncratic risk/return parameters. I've seen many advisers make the mistake of starting off by asking clients about their risk tolerance. Clients don't really know how to respond—and might not tell the whole truth even if they did. They're likely to tell you what they think you want to hear or what seems consistent with the persona or image they'd like to cultivate. In my experience, any *a priori* risk-tolerance statements from the client are unreliable or even misleading.

Consequently, I strongly encourage advisers to discard the often-used risk-tolerance questionnaires. The only merit to such exercises is perhaps in having a piece of paper that demonstrates that you actually talked to your client about risk, but there are better methods and more convincing evidence to use if you ever actually need it to defend your professional actions. Instead, it's better to perform the basic financial-planning exercise of determining the resources needed to meet the client's objectives (commonly called a capital-needs analysis) and use those conclusions to determine the required investment returns. Only then can you translate what you've learned into the *required* level of risk the client must be willing to tolerate. If the client can't learn to tolerate that degree of risk, the only real alternative is to change objectives (lesser expense, later retirement, reduced gifts to family or charity, et cetera). In our experience, few clients are willing to lower their financial expectations; they're willing, instead, to accept a higher level of risk—often far more—than they would have let on at a first meeting. Risk tolerance, in our experience, is a *derived conclusion* from careful analysis of client objectives; it's not a reliable initial input. And it can be learned; we've seen thousands of clients do it.

Consequently, concentration needs to be managed only if risk levels must be reduced. It can be maintained if the current levels of risk are, in fact, acceptable or if even greater levels of risk are necessary to accomplish the objectives your client truly wants to pursue. Be careful, therefore, not to assume that every concentrated stock situation is a problem to be solved. Many are, but some are not. For example, we work with a client—the chief executive officer of a public company—whose company stock makes up more than 85 percent of his net worth. The balance of that wealth, however, is more than $30 million and is broadly diversified across an array of assets not closely correlated to that company stock. If concentration like that is a problem, it's one most people would love to have.

The strategies presented in this book move from the simplest and fastest and, generally, lowest-cost solutions for reducing concentrated stock positions to the increasingly complex and often more-costly techniques. No one solution will be right for every client, and many of the techniques can be combined to accomplish clients' multiple objectives as well as to hedge against the potential for downside results that each of these strategies carries.

Another of our clients, for example, had a very large holding of stock and options in the company he worked for and, after long deliberations, accepted our urgings to diversify the position. But that happened only after he became convinced he could pursue *many* approaches simultaneously. Once he gave himself permission to diversify, he was almost giddy with enthusiasm to try a little of everything. In short order, this client sold a large number of high-basis shares outright, exercised his lowest-priced stock options (and immediately sold the resulting stock), transferred substantial amounts of stock options to his children, and funded a multimillion-dollar private foundation with his lowest-basis shares. This was hardly the random search for an answer it may appear to be. The combination of tactics made a great deal of sense to this client, providing comfort that important progress would be made even if some of the techniques ultimately failed to measure up. In the end, the client still left himself with a very substantial position in the stock options—just in case the company's stock price increased. For this client to make any diversification progress at all, a many-faceted hedge was indispensable.

Let's consider, then, the approaches you can use—whether mundane or multilayered—to help your clients meet their objectives.

Chapter Notes

1. Most people acknowledge 1990 Nobel laureate Harry Markowitz, beginning with his "Portfolio Selection" paper (*Journal of Finance* 7, no. 1 [March 1952]), as the first in a long line of distinguished thinkers who, together, have given us modern portfolio theory. Diversification of investment holdings to reduce overall portfolio risk forms the core of this school of thought. William Sharpe, also the 1990 Economics Nobel laureate (with Markowitz and University of Chicago economist Merton Miller), introduced the capital asset pricing model (CAPM) in the early 1960s and with it the now-familiar concepts of systematic (market) risk and nonsystematic (company-specific) *diversifiable* risk.

Managing Concentrated Stock Wealth

PART I

Sales

CHAPTERS 1 THROUGH 6 focus on the many and complex barriers to managing concentration risk and the most fundamental techniques for dealing with concentrated stock: selling the stock and not buying more. The simplicity and immediacy of this response often stun clients—and their advisers. In all cases, it's the right place to start—and in many, it's where you can stop.

1 Constraints on Managing Concentration Risk

Clients face many constraints in addressing the risks of concentrated stock positions. Taxes, contractual limitations, legal requirements, employer mandates, and—perhaps trickiest of all—an array of psychological barriers all complicate the process. Third-party observers are often stymied as to why concentrated stock positions are such a challenge. To demystify things, let's walk a short distance in the shoes of those burdened by concentrated positions, get a feel for the shape of the obstacles they face, and uncover ways to surmount them.

Finding solutions to concentrated stock problems means navigating some dangerous shoals. In the following chapters, we'll examine many of these obstacles in far more detail. Indeed, real-life examples of these constraints and how Kochis Fitz has dealt with them form the core of the various management strategies explored throughout the book. But first, let's get a basic understanding of why concentrated wealth can be so difficult to manage.

Taxes

No less an authority than Supreme Court justice Oliver Wendell Holmes observed in *Superior Oil Co. v. State of Mississippi*[1] that every person has the right to minimize his exposure to tax and to take advantage of every opportunity to avoid tax liability. "The very meaning of a line in the law," said Holmes, "is that you may get as close to it as you can if you do not pass it." This completely legitimate, even laudable, tax avoidance must be distinguished from the criminal activity of tax evasion, such as not reporting income or reporting fraudulent information. Although evasion can sometimes be a strong temptation, no adviser, of course, can encourage or condone such behavior for clients. No one will find any suggestions in this book to encourage any violation of the tax or any other law. Plenty of lawful and effective strategies for managing concentration risk are available. There is no need to go beyond those boundaries.

Still, a deep vein of aversion to tax liability runs through our culture, particularly among those who, as least as they see it, created their own wealth. Many clients dread incurring tax liability so much that they will bear the significant (and sometimes even acknowledged) risk of concentration just to avoid it. This isn't always the case, of course; some clients are quite willing to bear the tax cost, seeing it as an acceptable and indeed small price to pay for their financial success. Some even go to the opposite extreme and see taxes as a vehicle for giving back to society as a whole. As one of my tax professors at the University of Michigan Law School, L. Hart Wright, often told his students, "The federal government is my favorite charity." We all believed that he meant it. In any event, it was important to hear him repeat it, giving his eager young law students the proper perspective on their future responsibilities: not to beat the system but to take pains to understand it and make sure it operates as intended.

But this tax-as-charitable-gift point of view is not the perspective that typically brings clients to your office—at least not those looking for solutions to their concentration problems. Instead, it's often their aversion to the income tax exposure that the concentrated position presents. They are often surprised to learn that the gift and estate tax regime can also come into play (sometimes to their advantage but often involving additional costs). Be careful not to overwhelm your client with too much tax detail up front. We've had several clients, not savvy about tax law, become frightened by the intricacies and retreat to their former comfort zone, abandoning, at least for a time, any attempt to seriously address the tax issues around managing concentration risk.

So once you have the client's attention—or are able to regain it—make sure you're in command of the facts about the client's concentrated position. Ask these key questions:

What kind of asset is it? Not every asset qualifies as a capital asset. Whether it is or isn't has to do with facts and circumstances specific to the client. To an art dealer, a painting may be a piece of inventory (no capital gain, but ordinary income at sale); to the art collector who buys it from that dealer, it may be a capital asset. What's more, some assets, like depreciable real estate, must have some or all of any prior depreciation recaptured at sale as ordinary income, with only the balance, if any, taxed as capital gain. And some categories of assets simply aren't eligible for the favorable 5 and 15 percent rates. Capital gains on gemstones and precious metals, for example, are taxed at the 28 percent maximum rate.

Does the holding qualify for long-term capital gains treatment? In general, if it's been held more than one year, the federal long-term capital gains rates apply:

♦ Five percent until the generally applicable ordinary income tax bracket exceeds 15 percent.

♦ Fifteen percent for gains that cause total taxable income to exceed that level.

If it has not been held that long, then it may be a short-term capital gain, subject to tax at ordinary income rates, but like a long-term gain, it can first be offset by capital losses before the tax rates actually apply. For example, if in one taxable year, your client has both a short-term capital gain of $100,000 and a long-term capital loss of $75,000, only the $25,000 net amount is taxed—but at ordinary income rates.

This illustrates the common strategy of taking any available tax losses—by selling loss positions—to offset gains that may be necessary to achieve the diversification of a concentrated stock position. Clients are prone to seeing each piece of their overall portfolio in isolation. Many are very happily surprised to realize that the tax burden of diversification is not so bad after all, once the available loss positions in their portfolio are taken into account.

State tax laws usually follow the same more-than-one-year rule if they provide a special capital gains rate. Some states tax capital gains just like any other form of income.

What is the basis? Income taxes are only a problem for concentrated positions if there is an actual capital gain in excess of the asset's basis. A longtime client retired as chief executive officer of a public company and was immediately approached by a large brokerage firm to participate in an exchange fund it was assembling. To the brokerage firm's surprise, the aggregate holding was at a loss. "Never mind," was the broker's reaction. Now, no longer constrained by his position as CEO, our client was finally free to simply sell, at no tax cost. He had no appetite for the constraints of an exchange fund (see chapter 14, "Exchange Funds").

Capital gains and losses are measured from the asset's basis. Generally this is the amount the client paid for it, but capital additions or depreciation can move the basis up or down. And concentrated positions often result from gifts or inheritances. Generally gifts carry over the basis of the donor, and under current law, transfers of assets at death carry the date-of-death value as the asset's basis in the hands of the recipient. If your client has a $10/share basis in stock now worth $100/share and gives that stock to a family member as a gift, that family member will then have the same $10/share basis. If, instead, the client died and willed the stock to that family member, then the basis for that family member would be $100/share.

In view of this, some clients believe it's wise to plan to hold a highly appreciated concentrated position until their death so the basis can be stepped up to the value at that time and thus eliminate any income tax on the gain. I'll have more to say about taxes and basis in chapter 2, "Sale and Diversification"; chapter 7, "Gifts to Family"; and chapter 9, "Gifts to Charity." For now, it's enough to say that waiting for basis step-up at death is rarely optimal even under the current basis rules. It will be even more unlikely to be a worthwhile strategy if the basis rules change in 2010, when the law is scheduled to change. At that time, there will be only a limited dollar amount of basis step-up, regardless of actual values, leaving the balance of assets with no step-up in basis. And, in any event, to achieve basis step-up, assets must be exposed to the federal estate tax. Those estate tax rates, when they apply, apply to the asset's *entire* value (capital gains rates only apply to the gain *portion*) and are much worse than the income tax rates, as high as 47 percent in 2005. Managing around that set of tax exposures is often even more urgent an issue for clients than dealing with the concentrated stock position.

What timing and location flexibility is available? The state tax on capital gains can be a very significant factor in determining when and where your client sells highly appreciated stock. The state tax is deductible in calculating regular federal taxes and can yield federal tax savings at a higher rate than the rate on the capital gain itself. This is possible if the client's ordinary income in the same tax year exceeds the state tax owed (or paid) on the capital gain and other taxable income. For example, assuming no special complications, in a state with a 5 percent tax on capital gain, the *total* capital gains tax would be 18.25 percent for a client in the highest tax bracket:

Federal tax	15.00%
State tax	5.00
Deduction for state tax (.35 × .05)	(1.75)
	18.25%

But special complications abound. The state tax is deductible in the year in which it is *paid*, not the year the liability for the tax arises. So you must be careful to determine whether it's better to pay some or all of the state tax in the current year or wait until the following April 15. Complicating things even more is the fact that state taxes are not deductible for the alternative minimum tax calculation and do not create a minimum tax credit to be used in some later year. Depending on the size and character of your client's *other* income in the year of the capital gain transaction and in the year that follows, state taxes may apply at their full force with no offset from federal tax savings.

This potential state tax burden often prompts thoughts of moving in advance of the sale to a state with low or no income tax. Many California clients (with a current capital gains tax as high as 10.3 percent) consider a move to Nevada, for example—a state with no income tax—until they contemplate all the factors that must be accomplished to make such a change of domicile legitimate (having a believable principal residence in the new state, mailing address, club memberships, religious congregation, driver's license, voting registration, et cetera). Quite a few clients plan such a move for their eventual retirement, but for clients still actively involved in creating wealth, it rarely works as a strategy for ameliorating a specific capital gain exposure. And to be clear, changing one's domicile would work only for an intangible asset, such as a concentrated stock position. The original, high-tax state would still collect its tax on the sale of local real estate or, in most cases, the sale of a privately held business operating in that state.

And taxes aren't the only menace.

Post-IPO Lockups and Other Market Considerations

The founding owners, directors, and senior managers of companies that issue public stock are usually subject to an agreed-upon period following an initial public offering (IPO) during which they may not sell any of the newly public stock. Six months is typical, though it may be as short as a few months or as long as a year. To the surprise of many, these lockup periods are not required by law but are part of the conventional practice of public offerings in U.S. markets. Lockups are part of the deal made by the issuing company with its investment bankers to induce the investment bank to sell the shares in the public market and to do so in a reasonably orderly fashion during the time that the stock's price may be most vulnerable to significant volatility.

The great scandals that occurred at the height of the IPO boom in 1999 and early 2000 were *not* quick profits on newly issued stock made by insiders but rather by their friends and family—that is, short-term holders who were not subject to those lockups. Of course, insiders of newly public Company A, who were subject to lockup on Company A shares, often received large purchase opportunities for newly public Company B stock, on which they could capture huge profits in the first day or two of trading. Whatever your point of view about the virtue or vice of such cozy arrangements, if your client holds a large position in Company A stock and can't sell it because of a lockup, your client may still have a problem in need of a solution.

The expiration of the lockup is usually not a complete solution. The market is well aware of how much stock is locked up, for whom, and for how long, and can of course anticipate sales pressure once the lockup is lifted. Moreover, if the stock is subject to SEC Rule 144 and other notice requirements, your client has to inform the market in advance of an intention to sell. So even a client that is now free by law and by contract to sell shares may be unwilling to allow the expectation of the sale itself to depress the market price. Many believe that sales should occur slowly and gradually to minimize the market impact.

Realistically, however, most clients' purchases or sales of stock rarely if ever have an effect on the market price of the stock. The transactions are just too small, relative to the overall volume of trades, to have any noticeable effect on the price. For example, Microsoft traded more than 70 million shares on an average day in mid-2004. Even just 1 percent of that, or 700,000 shares, would amount to more than $17 million at the fifty-two-week low price of Microsoft stock at that time. Unless your client is Bill Gates, it's unlikely that your transaction could have a market impact on Microsoft's price.

Large holdings of much smaller companies, however, with much thinner trading volumes, could be affected by your client's transactions. Consequently, in those cases, you should help your client plan to sell at a measured pace, consistent with prevalent trading volumes and using limit orders to eliminate the risk of unacceptable market price declines.

Not all the implications of such transactions are negative. Another practical implication for large trades of concentrated stock is the opportunity to negotiate low transaction costs with the brokerage firm that will execute the trades. Consistent with many examples of economic efficiency that provide cost-control benefits, very large stock transactions offer the opportunity to negotiate a volume discount. Brokers are often willing to accept as little as one or two cents per share to sell very large blocks of stock ($500,000 in value is a reasonable threshold for "large" in this context). Sometimes, especially for new accounts, they'll do the sale for free, expecting plenty of business in the form of transactions for the proceeds of the concentrated stock sale.

SEC Constraints and the Sarbanes-Oxley Act

Helping your client meet the requirements of the securities laws and the still relatively new Sarbanes-Oxley Act of 2002 will be of great importance to advisers working with senior officers and directors of public companies. What follows is a quick overview of the five key elements that every adviser needs to understand regarding the constraints that securities and other laws impose on managing concentrated stock risk. Please note, however, that these rules are complex and some are quite new. Be sure to rely on competent legal counsel as you assist your clients with these issues. The legal officers of the companies involved in clients' concentrated stock positions are usually a very good resource for help in these matters.

Notice and Reporting

Some clients are among those large and influential shareholders who must give the market notice of the intent to sell their shares. This notice alerts the market not only to the potential sales volume but also to *who* is planning the sale. Immediately after the sale, the seller must publicly report the change in the stock ownership—again, so that the market is adequately informed. The corporation itself must be a party to this announcement, since it must approve the intended sale and it must forward information about the result to the Securities and Exchange Commission. Under Sarbanes-Oxley, any transaction in the company stock by these stockholders must be reported on SEC Form 4 almost immediately, that is, by the end of the second business day following the date of the transaction.

Controlled Sales of "Founder Stock"

Closely related to the notice and reporting requirements are the limitations imposed by Rules 144 and 145. For certain officers, directors, founders, et cetera, who acquire company stock by means other than open-market transactions, or whose stock is acquired by the company in a merger or acquisition, only so much stock can be sold, and only so frequently, into the public market (generally no more than 1 percent of the shares outstanding in any three-month period).

No Trading on Material, Nonpublic Information

Under Rule 10b5, no one may legally buy or sell stock based on important information about the company that is not publicly available. This sweeping restriction usually comes as a surprise to the lay investor. "Isn't that what smart investing is all about, being a step or two ahead of other investors?" Well, yes, if by that one means paying better attention to or making more insightful interpretation of *public* information. But it is illegal (both civil and criminal penalties can apply) to trade on information that the public market just doesn't have. Senior corporate executives and corporate directors routinely possess just such information about their companies and, consequently, are not permitted to transact for as long as that situation prevails. No one else in possession of that nonpublic information may do so either. A friend, a relative, even someone reading a crumpled scrap of paper tossed into a wastebasket is equally constrained. The notion of a legitimate "hot tip" is part of the fantasy lore of investment, not an opportunity permitted under the law. Martha Stewart was accused of just such a violation.

No "Short-Swing" Profits for Corporate Insiders

Under Rule 16b, certain senior corporate executives, directors, and very large stockholders, are considered insiders of the company and aren't permitted to keep profits that occur as a result of sales and purchases of shares within six months of each other. If such a set of transactions produces a profit, it belongs to the corporation and must be recovered from the offending insider.

Certain kinds of acquisitions (for example, stock-option exercises) are generally exempt from being considered purchases. But an open-market purchase precludes a sale of a corresponding volume of shares for at least six months. People subject to this rule usually have a great deal at stake in avoiding bad publicity, so *any* market purchase, however small, effectively precludes *any* sale for at least six months. If your client needs to sell a concentrated position, make sure he doesn't do any additional buying, at least not for more than six months before or after.

In a similar vein, Sarbanes-Oxley now prohibits corporate insiders from buying or selling company stock during any period in which employees generally are "blacked out" from making investment changes in their 401(k) or other retirement plans. These blackout periods usually occur only when there is a change in plan administration, but at least in the past, these periods of investment paralysis for employees have sometimes been fairly long. Now, at least with regard to transactions in the company stock, the senior executive ranks must be equally constrained.

No Favorable Financing for Senior Executives

Before the Sarbanes-Oxley law was enacted in 2002, it was common practice for public companies to provide large loans, under reasonably favorable terms, to senior executives to facilitate the purchase of company stock or exercise of options or to provide general liquidity for executives to compensate for their continuing to hold the stock. Companies may no longer directly provide—or arrange for a third party to provide—financing that is not available to employees generally.

Employment/Career Constraints

Many companies expect their directors to hold a minimum value of the company's stock. This expectation is rarely a major challenge for directors because the amount is usually not very substantial and the director status is a voluntary proposition for people who are typically fairly well to do.

But that's not necessarily the case for senior executives of those companies. For senior officers, the expectation is more of a *requirement* and the amounts are usually large, perhaps many times the executive's annual cash compensation. Similarly, in the wake of the Enron, WorldCom, and other executive abuses, companies are increasingly establishing formal stock-compensation arrangements that require long holding periods. Now that the Sarbanes-Oxley legislation has eliminated the practice of providing company loans, usually with very favorable terms, to facilitate acquiring and holding these large stock positions, the burden has increased twofold.

Even when there are no formal requirements to hold company stock, there is often an informal—but very clear—expectation of concentrated stock exposure as a condition of career success. On several occasions, I've met with cold refusals from CEOs in response to my advice not to own quite so much of their company's stock, and I've nearly been thrown out of more than one CEO's office for pointing out that their subordinate officers can afford the concentration risk even less.

It's important to recognize that there are several legitimate arguments in favor of corporate executives having concentration in their company's stock. Stock analysts, the investing public, and, more recently, politicians are eager to make sure that senior corporate officers have their fortunes closely linked to durable financial results for the corporation's shareholders. This notion of common financial interest has always been at the core of stock-based compensation arrangements. The newer elements speak to the *durability* of that alignment. In reaction to the extreme cases of senior corporate executives capturing vast wealth on short-term price spikes, the prevailing trend today is to force executives to hold stock for much longer terms.

As appealing as such strictures may appear on the surface, they create a giant disparity between the investment flexibility of those corporate executives and all other shareholders of the corporation's stock, who, wisely or not, can sell at any time. Executives are forced to accept a risk that no other shareholder faces. As a consequence, the overall investment exposure (risk *and* return) of shareholders and executives is not really aligned.

But the bigger problem lies in the potentially damaging effect on corporate decision making itself. Not every decision about corporate opportunity or threat will reflect the long view. If the senior decision makers are forced to hold very large holdings of the company's stock, their decisions may take a decidedly short-term, "play it safe" tone, especially because the Sarbanes-Oxley law makes the chief executive and chief financial officer personally liable for the "appropriate" and "fair" presentation of the company's financial condition in "all material respects" in the company's financial statements. Shareholders in general might benefit more in the long term by the decision makers' greater willingness to take risks in the short term. Corporate decision makers with disproportionate amounts of their wealth tied up in the company's stock may be—albeit subconsciously—unwilling to take those risks.

Helping your corporate executive clients find the right balance for their own portfolios will mean helping them to manage the challenge of these increasingly prevalent, and increasingly onerous, constraints.

Chapter 16, on opportunistic concentration, will address the other side of this coin, using employer stock concentration as a deliberate career-advancing strategy.

Psychological Barriers

People's general psychological framework, of course, influences all their decisions. This is no less true in the realm of investment and becomes especially apparent when it comes to acknowledging the risk of stock concentration. Many clients have significant blind spots about a *particular* stock holding even though they would scoff at the foolishness of holding any major position in many other stocks.

Richard Thaler, Terrance Odean, and other behavioral theorists[2] have observed the "legacy effect," "anchoring," and other irrational behaviors of many investors who cling to investment holdings only because they are familiar. In our experience, the resistance to change is especially pronounced when the holding is a true legacy. "My grandfather willed these shares to me; they've been in the family forever." Or, "My husband always handled these investments; we always did well." In such situations, achieving diversification is greatly complicated by the powerful emotions of affection, gratitude, and grief. Although clients will rarely admit it, many are unwilling to show disrespect for their benefactor's investment wisdom or ingratitude for their generosity by daring to sell the position. Others are simply convinced that the benefactor knew best.

In one case, we saw this kind of bias actually written into the provisions of an irrevocable trust. Two clients, both in their 20s, were the beneficiaries of an irrevocable trust established by their mother, who died when they were both quite young. For some reason that's no longer clear, the trust provided that its largest holding by far, a broadly traded very-large-cap domestic stock, could not be sold by the trustee prior to any trust distribution. We used puts in other, nontrust assets (see chapter 15 on derivatives) and a tax-managed account, set to avoid purchasing any more of this stock (see chapter 13 on index-proxy management), to moderate this risk while the trust distributions were pending. We encouraged these clients to rapidly diversify this holding as soon as installment distributions occurred at ages 25, 30, and 35. These young clients were victims not of their own psychological impediments but of their mother's (or of her advisers', who had long since left the scene).

Anchoring, another form of dysfunctional investment psychology, is the belief that somehow the market is aware of the investor's historic, higher price for the stock and owes him a recovery to that price. Some clients just can't sell at a loss. Despite the financial benefits of capturing a capital loss for tax purposes, selling a position below the original cost confirms a failure that such clients are loath to admit. When the potential risk that concentration presents—loss of value—in fact occurs, it can paralyze clients. The lower the price goes, the more convinced of a recovery they become. To keep clients from falling prey to such faulty thinking, advisers should urge them to set boundaries for the tolerable price declines of concentrated positions. Boundaries should be tied to the required remaining value necessary to accomplish the client's crucial objectives. Once the boundary is reached, the client should be committed to selling, to avoid even greater, unaffordable losses.

The investment maxim that over time, broadly diversified equity portfolios must increase to reflect long-term fundamental economic growth does *not* apply to any *one* company. Poor management, lack of innovation, aggressive competition, or just plain bad luck can cause any company to just limp along or even fail—even in the midst of a generally robust, growing economy.

Another troublesome blind spot afflicts many corporate employees at all levels, not just the senior executives who may be compelled to own large positions in an employer's stock. For novice investors, the tendency may reflect a lack of awareness of the many investment alternatives available. So many companies make purchase of their stock broadly available, through discounted stock-purchase plans, 401(k) matching contributions, restricted stock, and stock options, that the first stock most people ever own is probably the stock of the company they work for. These ready-made opportunities to acquire stock combine with a natural sense of team spirit to cause most employees to end up with a far larger share of their employer's stock in their total portfolio than any objective investor would think wise. What's more, the employees take pride in this choice. The stock price debacles of Enron, WorldCom, and others haven't cured this dangerous myopia. In 2004, the prevalence of company stock in 401(k) plans was still 16 percent[3] (down only a little from 19 percent at the end of 2000). So, in the worst case, the collapse of a company can destroy an employee's job, threaten retirement plan assets, and devastate the employee's portfolio all at the same time.

Such overweighting is by no means limited to the naive rank and file. Many otherwise sophisticated, experienced, and wealthy corporate executive clients remain convinced that their company's stock represents an investment opportunity that surpasses any alternative. They may, of course, be right, but your clients cannot trust their instincts here. They are too close to the trees of their own company and its industry to see the forest that other, objective investors see. Their very connection to—and even dependence on—their company's current investment performance and their intimate familiarity with its plans for the future can be an investment handicap. The stock price doesn't hinge on what your client knows about the company, but on what all of those millions of other potential investors around the world *think* they know about it.

A few years ago, our firm worked with a number of executives at a company whose stock had been advancing at a market-beating rate for a number of years. (This was a very well established, "old economy" company, not some flimsy dot-com IPO.) These clients were becoming rich, of course, and increasingly optimistic about the stock's future—and all the more impatient with our urgings to diversify. Eventually, a news report of misstated earnings in a then recently acquired subsidiary caused the stock to decline by 50 percent—in one day. It has never recovered. Needless to say, this was not the way to reduce ongoing concentration risk.

Chapter Notes

1. 280 U.S. 390 (1930).

2. Thaler, Richard. *The Winner's Curse: Paradoxes and Anomalies of Economic Life,* Free Press, 1991 (Princeton University Press paperback, 1993).

Thaler, Richard. "The End of Behavioral Finance," *Financial Analysts Journal,* AIMR, November/December 1999.

Odean, Terrance. "Are Investors Reluctant to Realize Their Losses?" *Journal of Finance,* October 1998.

Shefrin, Hersh. *Beyond Greed and Fear: Understanding Behavioral Finance and the Psychology of Investing.* Boston, MA: Harvard Business School Press, 1999.

3. Employee Benefit Research Institute/Investment Company Institute database for more than 45,000 401(k) plans as of December 31, 2003.

2 Sale and Diversification

The classic "efficient frontier" of modern portfolio theory identifies a concentrated stock position as suboptimal—having too much risk for the expected return or not enough return for the expected risk (see ***Figure 2.1***). Moving to the frontier of opportunity can produce less risk, more return, or both by diversifying the holding. But this theoretical approach to improving investment outcomes often leaves clients cold, with only tepid motivation to overcome the many obstacles to addressing the risks of concentrated wealth. It also leaves them vaguely apprehensive that they might be abandoning the possibility of exceptional returns if that concentrated stock ultimately does very well.

Comprehensive wealth managers can be especially helpful to clients facing such choices by putting the whole question into context. What resources are necessary to accomplish the client's complete array of goals? Careful analysis of this question permits advisers to judge how much of the client's total financial resources is crucial to achieving those objectives and how much, if any, is in excess of what's really necessary. Any excess wealth can be devoted to expanded goals, to gifts, or to investments with degrees of risk that would not be tolerable for the core portfolio.

FIGURE 2.1 **The Efficient Frontier**

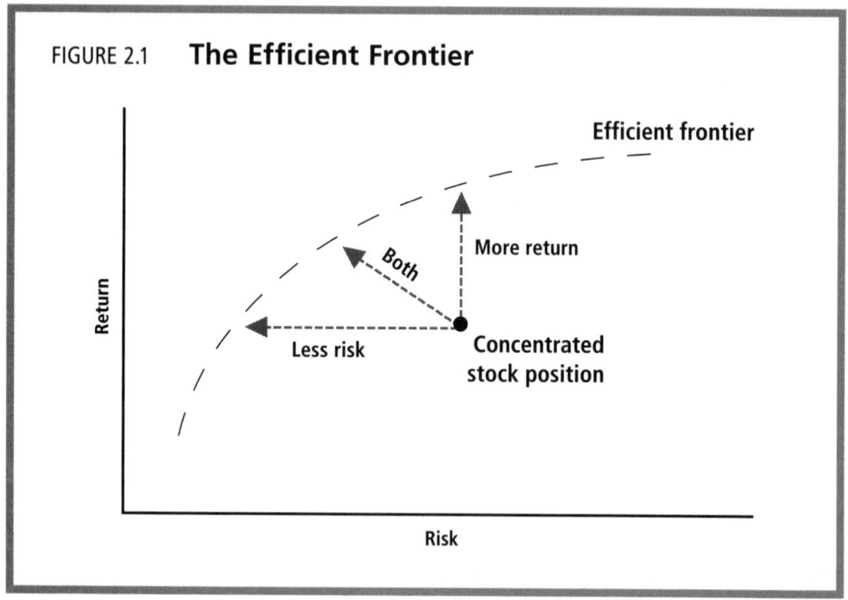

Clients with concentrated stock positions are sometimes among those fortunate people who do have excess resources. But when they see, perhaps for the first time, that they can indeed *afford* concentration risk, some nevertheless begin to wonder why they should continue to take that particular risk. Why not tolerate the permissible risk in some other area—perhaps taking a chance on something more fun or more satisfying, like funding a trendy new restaurant, patronizing a promising young artist, developing a vineyard property, or investing in something that has even greater potential return than is likely for the concentrated stock? Paraphrasing the fundamental message of the investment theory, clients often say things like, "Whew, it's good to know I can afford this risk, but why should I take it for only so-so returns? Let's go all out."

Most clients, however, even wealthy ones, almost invariably have objectives that will use up all the resources they can muster—and maybe then some. For them, seeing the reality of their need for more-reliable investment results provides the imperative for diversification that might otherwise never have captured their attention.

For either group, then, the first and often easiest step in dealing with the concentrated position is simply to sell it and put the proceeds to work somewhere else. It is often that straightforward.

Overcoming the Tax Constraint

In the sale of concentrated stock, taxes are most often the chief obstacle to overcome. But even in the worst case, when the owner has zero basis in the asset, the maximum rate of federal tax on long-term capital gain is now 15 percent, leaving at least 85 percent of the asset available to invest elsewhere. With any basis, of course, the tax bill comes down and the after-tax proceeds available increase, as shown in ***Figure 2.2***.

Clients can overcome their aversion to the *concept* of the tax liability once you focus them on the actual tax burden instead. Many new clients arrive in our office convinced that they can't sell, for fear of taxes, and they're determined not to be dissuaded from that view. Indeed, on several occasions, new clients have announced early on: "You won't get me to sell that position." Clients often fear that advisers may be just a bit too professionally detached. After all, we don't bear the tax burden; our clients do. Still, they usually imagine the tax burden to be far worse than it actually is. The capital gains tax burden was once much more onerous than it is today, and some

FIGURE 2.2 **Basis and the Tax Bite**

Basis as % of Asset Value	Federal Tax as % of Asset Value	Net Diversified Proceeds
0	15.00%	85.00%
25%	11.25	88.75
50	7.50	92.50
75	3.75	96.25

Source: Kochis Fitz

FIGURE 2.3 **Expected Returns**

	Concentrated	Diversified
Prospective return	30%	10%
Probability	× 25%	× 90%
Risk-adjusted return rate	7.5%	9%

Source: Kochis Fitz

clients can remember an effective rate of 49.125 percent—just for federal tax on capital gains—in the mid-1970s. Old beliefs die hard. A patient explanation of how small the tax cost is now can be very helpful. Ultimately, most clients can shrug off a tax bill—at least one they consider small enough—especially if you encourage them to do just that.

But overcoming that psychological barrier is only the first step. The destination for the sale proceeds has to be more appealing than just staying put. That, of course, is the goal of diversification: a greater risk-adjusted, or expected, return for a diversified portfolio than for a concentrated position. In the simplest terms, suppose the concentrated position promises a return of 30 percent but has only a 25 percent chance of accomplishing it, and the diversified alternative promises only a 10 percent return but has a 90 percent probability of success. For a client who can't afford the risk of the concentration, the diversified alternative seems more appealing (see ***Figure 2.3***).

But what about those taxes? For example, if your client has only 85 percent (worst case) of the pretax value to work with, the attraction of diversification appears to get very slim (see ***Figure 2.4***).

Be careful not to let your clients fall into a conceptual trap here. It is generally not appropriate to compare the return potential of the existing, *pretax* position with the return potential of the *after-tax* proceeds of sale. That inappropriate analytical shortcut could lead clients to require the diversified alternative to offer a higher prospective return. The benefit of diversification comes from reducing risk;

FIGURE 2.4 **Expected Returns After Tax on Sale**

	Concentrated	**Diversified**
Amount generating return	100%	85%
Risk-adjusted return rate	× 7.5%	× 9%
Risk-adjusted expected return	7.5%	7.65%

Source: Kochis Fitz

therefore, the only fair comparison is between *risk-adjusted* return potentials.

What's more, the apparent tax disadvantage of the diversified alternative, as small as it might be, is still probably overstated. That's because, barring a step-up in basis at the client's death, that tax burden must eventually occur. The choice is not really between tax and diversified returns versus no tax and concentrated returns, but rather between being taxed now or taxed later.

Deferring tax is generally a good idea, all other things being equal. But all other things are *not* equal here. Future tax rates could well be different. Some clients hope for even lower rates, but many fear that rates will be higher. And throughout any period of deferring tax by deferring sale, driven by a client's belief in rates eventually becoming lower, that tax-optimistic client must still bear the higher risk of the concentrated position. You can help your client put this in proper perspective by analyzing how much tax rates would have to decline—and how soon—to justify continuing to bear the concentration risk (see ***Figure 2.5***).

This analysis can readily test the all-too-common belief that it's worth waiting for basis step-up at death. That belief is simply a matter of expecting the tax rate on the client's holding to decline to zero. Extending the examples in Figure 2.5, that would require, at most, a timeframe of twelve years for a risk-adjusted return differential of a mere 1.5 percent. If the differential in favor of diversification is greater or if the current tax burden is smaller, it takes less time to

FIGURE 2.5 **Return Differentials: Example 1**

Expected return differential: 1.5%, in favor of diversification
Net diversifiable proceeds: 85% (that is, zero basis and 15% tax rate)

Potential future tax rate on current taxable gain	Years until diversified proceeds break even with existing concentrated position
10%	5
5	8
0	12

Return Differentials: Example 2

Expected return differential: 3%, in favor of diversification
Net diversifiable proceeds: 92.5% (that is, 50% basis and 15% tax rate)

Potential future tax rate on current taxable gain	Years until diversified proceeds break even with existing concentrated position
10%	1
5	2
0	3

Source: Kochis Fitz

break even. If your client's death is imminent, postponing sale could be wise. In fact, however, most clients who come to you with concentrated stock positions will be decades away from their final years.

Consequently, waiting for basis step-up is almost always a flimsy rationale for not selling. It will be even less persuasive if the currently scheduled change in the rules for basis step-up (a limited actual dollar amount of step-up to be assigned to specific assets, not an unlimited, across the board benefit) actually goes into effect in 2010. What's more, even today, shares of company stock distributed from certain qualified employer plans don't qualify for basis step-up at all (see chapter 16).

Overcoming Psychological Barriers

Of course, taxes aren't the only problem. Both the legacy effect and anchoring—the emotional or psychological perspectives that keep clients from being consistently rational about their investment—can have a powerful hold.

Some years ago, a new client presented us with her existing portfolio. The standout holding was a large position in a major local company. "How did you wind up buying so much of that stock?" I asked.

"I didn't," she explained. "My father was once the company's chief executive officer; he gave me those shares long ago and urged me to hold them. That company and those shares have been part of my life for a long time."

"But that stock hasn't done much in quite a while, and even the dividend is not that large."

"Oh, I don't get the dividends; I've had the dividends automatically reinvested from the start. That was my father's idea, too," she proudly announced.

"How long ago was that?"

"About twenty-five years; it's really grown a lot."

Anticipating the nightmare of calculating the actual basis of this holding (the original gift carrying the father's basis and each subsequent dividend buying additional fractional shares over many years), we were tempted to leave bad enough alone. But this client truly needed this part of her portfolio to perform, and the existing holding offered little promise. Our long-range capital-adequacy analyses convinced her of the *need* to sell, but giving herself permission to do so took more than data.

We explained that her father, long deceased, and his team were no longer in control of the company. The world had moved on, and if her father were still living, his assessment probably would have changed as well. In any event, after all this time, he'd want her to be free to make decisions that were right for her, here and now. The clincher to getting her to sell was a plan to hold back 1,000 shares (including those we couldn't find basis for) to give to her father's favorite charity as a gift in his honor and memory.

Sometimes the key to convincing the client to decide to sell is a new investment opportunity. For several years, we worked with a client who held numerous directorships in a particular industry and had been CEO of one of the larger firms in that business. He had also been an investor in several broad venture-capital investment partnerships. His biggest venture win was a $1 million–plus position in Cisco Systems, with a basis of just a few dollars. Repeated attempts to encourage him to cash in his winnings—even reminding him that the famous venture investors who ran the fund had long since captured *their* profits and moved on—failed to budge him.

One day, he was entertaining himself—and us—with his view that his industry was a very good long-term reflector of the growth of the economy, with little downside risk because of its strong and always durable consumer demand. "Owning four or five of the main companies in this industry really can't go wrong as a long-term portfolio strategy," he opined.

We had our opening.

"Okay, then, why don't we take your Cisco position and sell it to put your money where your belief is? What do *you* know about Cisco or its opportunities and risks that many, many others don't know better? You *do* know a lot about your own industry; let's buy that instead." We did, the next day. Once his initial reluctance to selling Cisco was overcome, we had permanently crossed his diversification boundary. Within the next six months, we were able to further diversify those still-large replacement positions with no continuing objection.

ESOP Sales

A special case of managing concentrated stock ownership can apply to a privately owned company. Under current tax provisions (Internal Revenue Code Section 1042), the owners of a closely held company can sell part or all of their interest to a special qualified plan—called an employee stock ownership plan (ESOP)—for the benefit of their employees. This strategy can provide several benefits, including tax-deferred earnings for the employees as well as tax-deferred gains for the initial owners who are selling.

As long as the seller's proceeds are reinvested in U.S. securities within two years, taxes on that sale are deferred, possibly for many years, until those replacement assets are themselves sold. To achieve the benefits of diversification for those proceeds—without concern over capital gains taxes each time a transaction in the diversified portfolio might be necessary—we've used very long-term, noncallable, high-quality corporate bonds as the replacement property for the former closely held business asset. That fixed-income replacement property may not provide the potential for lower risk and higher return that your client is looking for. But long-term, noncallable bonds can be collateral for margin borrowing (see chapter 12). The proceeds of that margin can be used to purchase investments with higher return potential, such as a diversified equity portfolio. The client is then free to later sell those diversified assets without triggering the large deferred gains from the initial ESOP sale. Those gains are housed in the fixed-income assets purchased as the replacement for the company ownership. There is no expectation of transacting in those high-quality, long-term, noncallable bonds for perhaps decades to come.

Let's Just Sell It

So, it turns out, simply selling the position is often the best answer. The next several chapters deal with special considerations for corporate employees, especially senior executives, who commonly face the concentration problem. For them, just selling is often not simple at all.

3 Coordinating Long Shares With Stock Options

Senior corporate executives are among the clients most likely to have concentrated stock positions. The positions usually include both shares held outright (long shares) and shares under restriction, as well as shares that they may acquire under employee stock options. Chapter 6 focuses on restricted stock; in this chapter, we'll address the task of managing the *combination* of long shares and stock options.

Owning a large or potentially large holding of company stock is not necessarily a problem. It's an issue only if the concentration risk undermines the likelihood that your client will accomplish all his core objectives. If your client is confident of accomplishing core objectives, notwithstanding the concentrated position, he's free to accept its risk. Indeed, accepting that risk may be helpful, even essential, to accomplishing his discretionary, ambitious objectives. Chapter 16 explores this notion of opportunistic concentration in more detail. For now, it's enough to recognize that the combination of stock options and long shares is often what enables your corporate executive client to have it both ways.

Employee Stock Options

Employee stock options are granted to corporate directors and employees as a form of compensation for services. Although options have many critics, most people believe they provide a number of special advantages, both to the option recipients and to the corporate employer and its shareholders. Options are almost always granted with an exercise price equal to the value of the stock on the date of grant. Then for some period of time, usually ten years (or less in the event of death, retirement, or termination), the option grantee can exercise at that usually fixed price. Thus, option holders reap financial gain only if the stock price increases—and only in the same amount and at the same time as that gain occurs for shareholders generally (see ***Figure 3.1***). Theoretically at least, the interests of the owners (shareholders) of the company are in line with the interests of the hired staff (option holders) and that staff

FIGURE 3.1 **The Dynamics of a Stock Option**

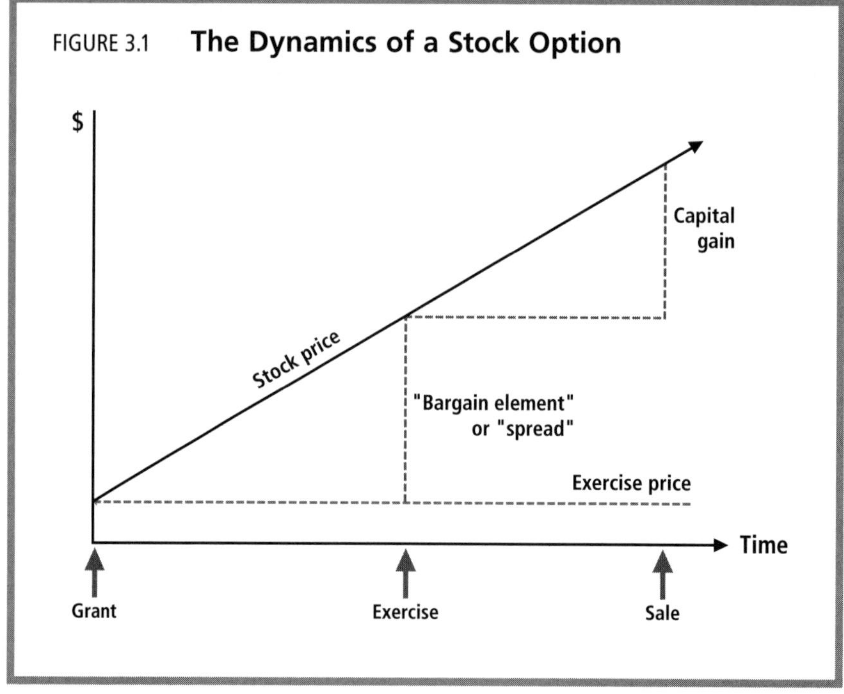

Source: Kochis Fitz

is given strong incentive to enrich the shareholders as they enrich themselves.

The features of stock options vary widely, which explains the need for using "almost always" and "usually" in describing how they work. Some are granted at prices below or above the stock's market value at grant date; others last more or less than ten years. They may vest (be exercisable) immediately and all at once or only after some lapse of time and then only in installments. Some options automatically replace themselves (reload) when exercised; others have gradually increasing exercise prices. The variations don't stop there. This is a compensation device, after all, and there is no limit to the creativity of employers and employees in designing programs to accommodate specific needs, competitive pressures, and respective negotiating strengths.

Strong debate continues about the merits of stock options. The concern is focused mainly on perceived option abuses in a number of notorious cases of corporate misconduct. The debate gets especially heated when it touches on the merits—or faults—of requiring companies to account for the expense of options. Entering that debate here wouldn't add to advisers' ability to understand and respond to the risks and opportunities of concentrated wealth for corporate executives and directors. If stock options continue as a robust compensation device—and I believe they will—then those risks and opportunities will continue to present management challenges to advisers. If options gradually fall out of favor, then the specific problems that options add to the concentration dilemma gradually solve themselves. (See the sidebar on the following two pages.)

Taxes on Options

Employee stock options come in two varieties: nonqualified stock options (NQSOs) and incentive stock options (ISOs). The tax treatment of NQSOs is straightforward; let's start there. As long as the NQSO is granted with an exercise price equal to or greater than the stock's fair market value on the date of grant, the recipient has no tax liability at the time of grant. Although the stock price may

To Expense or Not to Expense? That's Not the Question

ALMOST ALL COMMENTATORS are calling for the expensing of employee stock options. And, barring congressional action to intervene, the Financial Accounting Standards Board (FASB) plans to *require* expensing by all public companies in 2005. The real issue, however, is not whether, but when and how to actually accomplish this.

Many companies object to expensing because they object to the currently preferred methodology for valuation—the Black-Scholes option-pricing model. That model won a Nobel Prize for its authors in 1973 and has enjoyed wide acceptance in the financial community with respect to its original purpose of estimating a value of the future economic opportunity presented by a *market* option. The original purpose of the Black-Scholes pricing model relates to an option that can be transacted in the marketplace. Typical employee stock options cannot be transacted in the marketplace at all. Many of them can't even be given away to family members.

The Black-Scholes model was designed to deal with the pricing of options that have a relatively short duration: three months, six months, or nine months, at most. Employee stock options can last for ten years. The factors used in the Black-Scholes model—volatility of stock price and interest rates—can produce dramatic distortions if they're extended over the long stretch of time an employee option's potential exercise period is in effect. The value of an employee stock option, however, can be destroyed or greatly diminished instantly by termination of the holder's employment or by the death of the holder. Such events do not affect market options. Market options last for as long as they last and cannot be altered or destroyed. Consequently, many see the Black-Scholes model as an extremely poor valuation device for employee stock options. It's a bad fit.

This debate presents an excellent opportunity for the compensation-consulting profession to explore alternative ideas for valuing employee stock options. Consultants in this field routinely design and install stock-option programs and have access to—and significant credibility with—corporate executives and compensation committees of boards. Their shoulders should be broad enough for them to enter the fray and come up with a uniform methodology for valuing options that accommodates the many peculiarities of employee stock options. With an appropriate valuation methodology in place, the investing public can make meaningful comparisons. "Company A spent X dollars on options, and over time, it achieved Z results. Company B spent Y dollars on options, and over time, it achieved 2 times Z results." Right now, such comparisons are not possible. They should be, and they should be reliable.

In fact, meaningful comparisons are now very difficult because of the tremendous potential for distortion from company to company, depending on whether each is required to recognize the cost of options at the time of grant or at the time serial vesting occurs. Timing is a significant problem for any valuation methodology and one that has not yet received adequate attention. One workable solution may be to account for the options (by whatever methodology) *tentatively,* at the time of grant. Then, at a later date, when and if the options are ever exercised or if they expire unexercised, there would be a reconciliation. On the date of exercise (or on the date that an unexercised option expires), there is either a cost to the employer or no cost at all. The cost is the difference between what the option holder pays at exercise and what someone in the marketplace would have to pay for that share of stock at that time. That difference in value received by the company in exchange for the stock is the most clearly measurable, real cost to the employer, and it occurs only when an option is exercised for less than the stock's market value.

Assume, for example, a $10 exercise price and an eventual $15 fair market value per share of stock at the time of exercise. The company could take that share of stock to the marketplace on the date of exercise and receive $15 for it. On that date, the true cost of the option—$5 ($15 market value less the $10 exercise price)—is finally known. Looking back, did the company recognize the cost of that option correctly? What if the company estimated a cost of $3 at the date of grant? That means it counted only part of the actual cost. Now, the company should take another $2 of cost into account (leaving aside present/future value issues that could be built into the projection as well). Suppose the company recognized a cost at grant of $20. In that case, the company should receive a credit of $15 (again, taking time-value issues into account) because the true cost of the option turned out to be only $5.

In any case, if companies are required to recognize *something* on the date of grant, current and potential shareholders have some knowledge of the expense the company is *expecting* to incur, with reconciliation later once the true cost is actually known. If such a first-and-second-look regime were used, much of the remaining opposition to option expensing could disappear—even if no one is able to come up with something more appropriate than Black-Scholes.

increase over time, there is still no tax liability until the option holder exercises the option. At that point, the "bargain element," or spread (see Figure 3.1), is taxed as ordinary compensation income. Since this value is compensation, the employer is required to withhold income taxes, Medicare tax, and any FICA liability remaining to be paid for that tax year. With state taxes included, total withholding requirements can approach or even exceed 40 percent of the total income amount. This immediate tax burden provides strong incentive—aside from any desire to minimize concentration risk—to sell at least enough of the acquired shares virtually immediately to pay these taxes.

The shares acquired by exercising NQSOs have a basis equal to the amount paid (the exercise price) plus the amount of the taxable income. Thus, the exercise of an option to acquire stock at, say, $15 when the stock is trading at $20 yields a taxable event of $5 for each share and a subsequent basis of $20 in each acquired share. Like any other capital asset, when those shares are later sold—whether the same day or many years later—any increase or decrease in value is a long- or short-term gain or loss, depending on the length of that holding period.

ISOs are quite a bit more complex. Like almost all NQSOs, ISOs are not taxable when granted. Unlike NQSOs, ISOs are not permitted to be granted at a discount price. There are also restrictions on who may receive ISOs (only employees, not nonemployee directors or contractors) and ISOs may not be granted for a value that would cause more than $100,000 of exercise price to vest in any one year. Any excess is, by definition, an NQSO. In the 30,000-share grant example in ***Figure 3.2***, only 26,664 shares are ISOs; the remaining 3,336 are NQSOs. The example assumes an exercise price of $15 per share, with vesting of one-quarter of the shares (7,500) each year.

At the exercise of an ISO, no regular federal income tax is due; FICA and Medicare taxes, however, still apply. Nevertheless, the spread at exercise is an adjustment for the alternative minimum tax (AMT), which could still subject the exercise to taxation. That additional AMT liability is intended to be a *prepayment* of tax, not necessarily a permanent increment. That prepayment is achieved by

FIGURE 3.2 **ISOs or NQSOs?**

Year	No. of Shares Vesting	Total Exercise Value Vesting @ $15	AMOUNT PERMITTED TO BE ISOs: Value	AMOUNT PERMITTED TO BE ISOs: No. of Shares	Shares Vesting as NQSOs
1	7,500	$112,500	$100,000	6,666	834
2	7,500	112,500	100,000	6,666	834
3	7,500	112,500	100,000	6,666	834
4	7,500	112,500	100,000	6,666	834
	30,000			**26,664**	**3,336**

Source: Kochis Fitz

creating a credit for AMT attributable to a deferral preference, like the spread on an ISO exercise, which can be used in any subsequent year to reduce the regular tax bill to the level of the AMT in that year. Sometimes the credit value can be fully captured in the year immediately following, and the overall net cost amounts only to the time value of money for a fairly short period. Often—and this is increasingly the case for many clients—it can take many years to absorb this credit because the regular tax and the AMT calculations yield very close results, often with the AMT result higher, even without further ISO exercises. Thus the AMT attributable to an ISO exercise can, in fact, be a large, unrecoupable burden.

The basis for the stock acquired through an ISO also has complications. There are two different bases: one for regular tax purposes (the amount paid, or the exercise price) and the other for subsequent AMT calculations (the amount paid plus the amount of the adjustment for the spread). ***Figure 3.3*** on the following page shows the key tax characteristics for an ISO granted at $15 and exercised at a market value of $20.

FIGURE 3.3 **Tax Characteristics for an ISO**

FICA/ Medicare Taxable Base	Regular Taxable Income	AMT Preference Adjustment	BASIS	
			AMT	Regular
$5	0	$5	$20	$15

FIGURE 3.4 **Taxation of Initial $5 Spread at Exercise of an ISO**

	Regular Tax System	AMT
Taxable at exercise	0	$5
Taxable at sale	$5	0

Source, top and bottom: Kochis Fitz

It is important to recognize the special AMT basis so that the amount of the initial economic value is not taxed again under the AMT when the stock is later sold. The AMT always operates simultaneously with the regular tax, whether at the exercise of the option or at the sale of the stock. So, to avoid having that $5 of initial value spread ($20 – $15) taxed twice, the stock's AMT basis is increased by the amount taxed under the AMT at exercise, as indicated in ***Figure 3.4***.

The complications don't stop there. When the acquired stock is subsequently sold, the initial spread amount—and here is the big incentive—is taxed as a long-term capital gain for regular tax purposes *if* the stock is sold more than one year after the exercise *and* more than two years after the grant. If either of those time requirements is not met, a sale or a gift of ISO-acquired stock disqualifies those shares. The initial spread reverts to being ordinary compensation income—but in the year of the sale or gift. Any appreciation in value beyond the stock's price at the time of exercise is either a long- or short-term gain according to the normal holding-period rules.

Because of the rule that the sale must take place more than one year after exercise and two years after the grant, many ISO plans simply don't permit any exercise until the first anniversary of the grant, thus making it impossible not to meet both tests as long as either one is met. The better plan design, however, would permit immediate exercise following grant, allowing the normal twelve-month, long-term gains clock to start running as early as possible. This would accommodate the capture of early gains as long-term capital gains even if they were not very durable beyond that. For example, a client of ours was permitted under his ISO plan to exercise his option immediately after the grant. Within a few months, after some price appreciation, he did so. In the following twelve months, the price skyrocketed to a level we all feared couldn't be maintained. Rather than wait another nine months to meet the two-years-from-grant rule, we decided to sell, capturing most of the total gain as a long-term capital gain, deliberately sacrificing that treatment for the relatively small increase that had occurred early on before the exercise.

Of course, all of these complexities can be avoided. No one is required, at least not by tax law, to hold the ISO-acquired shares. Assuming your client is otherwise free to do so, she *can* sell (disqualify) the stock immediately upon exercise. If that sale occurs within the same calendar year, in fact, none of the strange AMT effects apply.

Still, the prospect of capital gains tax treatment is tantalizing and shouldn't be given up too easily. The relative advantages of capital gains versus ordinary income treatment should always be considered in the management decisions on all of the components of a concentrated stock position: long shares, restricted stock, NQSOs, and ISOs.

Exercise Strategies

Over many years of advising holders of employee stock options, Kochis Fitz has developed a comprehensive strategic approach to capitalizing on stock option opportunities. ***Figure 3.5*** is a decision tree diagramming the key features of this strategic architecture for stock options. The left side of the diagram focuses on options as opportunistic wealth-building devices. We'll explore that side of the analytical framework in chapter 16. Our concern here is with the right side, where the goal of an option *exercise* is to sell the resulting stock either to fund some valuable near-term spending objective or to capture the concentrated stock value available in the option and put it to work in some other diversified investment.

When the goal is to accomplish a current spending objective, the prompt to action is fairly clear. When the after-tax value of exercise and sale would buy the desired result, your client should be prepared at least to consider taking action right then and there. When the motivation is the more theoretical one of reducing risk through diversification, the prompt is less clear, though still quite subjective. We always advise clients to set in advance some trigger for action. Sometimes, it's simply a function of time: a plan to exercise profitable options every January, for example. More typically, it's a financial trigger: when the bargain element equals a 50 percent bonus, or when that spread amounts to $50,000 or $100,000 or $1 million, et cetera. There is no magic number here; rather it's whatever level of incremental wealth your client would hate to jeopardize because of a decline in this stock's price. That measure, of course, can change over time and should be related to the size and character of the rest of your client's wealth. But whatever the trigger, once it's reached, the client is primed to take action. Short of that threshold, nothing need be done. It's just not worth the bother—not yet, at least.

Whatever the trigger that causes the stock-option diversification plan to go into effect, your client may still feel the remorse of selling a potentially winning investment. Consequently, you should calculate the future stock-price increases that would justify waiting to exercise and sell to adequately overcome the continuing risk of concentration. This determination puts objective parameters around the client's natural temptation to second-guess the initial decision to diversify. For example, if your client has an option at an exercise price of $10 when the stock is selling at $20 a share, her tax rate is 35 percent, and the likely diversified investment opportunity rate is 6 percent after

FIGURE 3.5 **Stock Option Strategy**

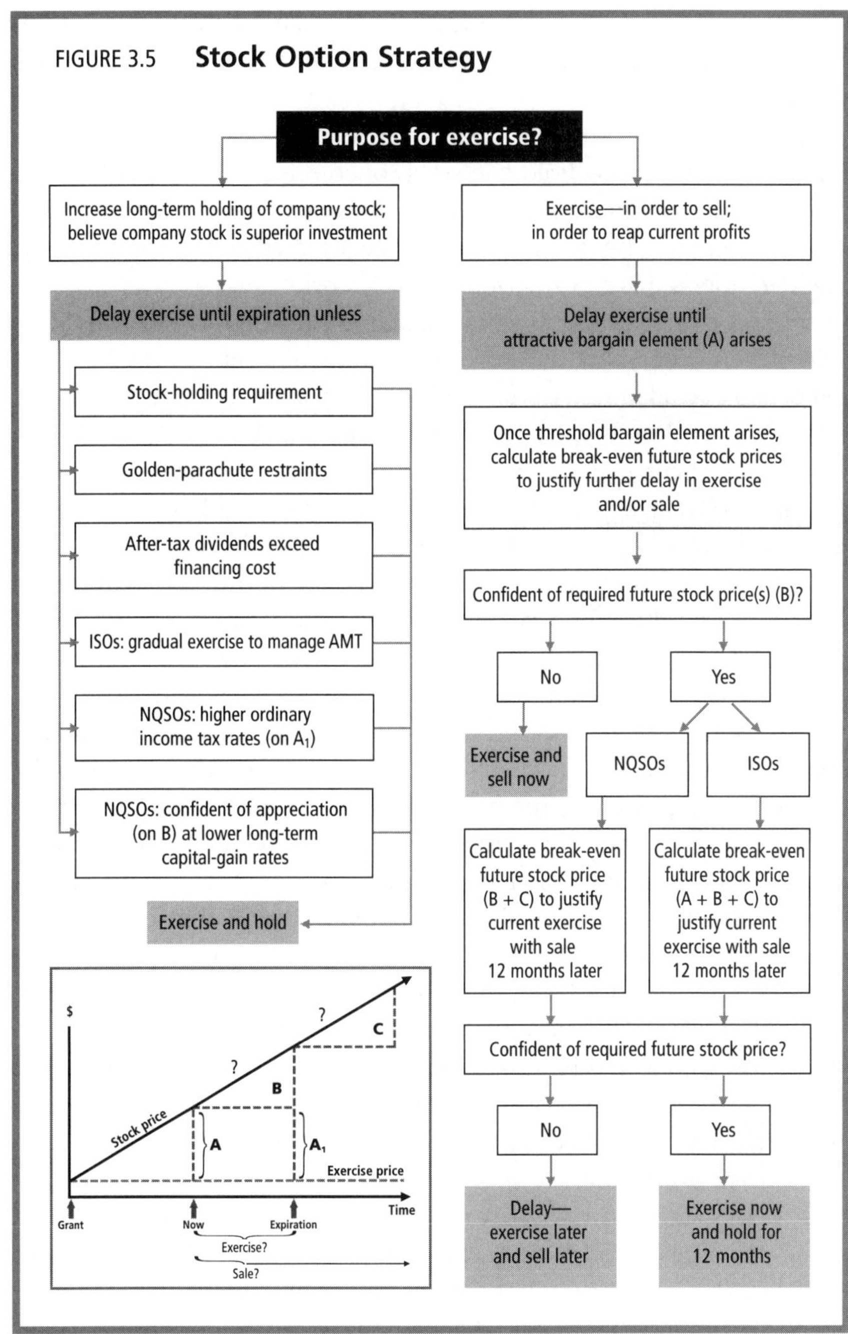

Source: Kochis Fitz © 2004

tax, the option's stock price would have to increase to at least $20.60 within a year, $21.92 in three years, or $23.38 in five years to make delay worthwhile.

Whether or not the stock pays a dividend is irrelevant here. Your client doesn't plan to hold the stock once acquired. The only question is when to exercise, with sale of the stock to take place immediately thereafter. There is no plan to collect a dividend in this strategy; the decision is driven only by the stock's price. Nevertheless, if your client is convinced that those calculated minimum future stock prices will indeed occur, then she should forgo the diversification; the client expects to be adequately compensated for the risk. If not convinced, however, she should exercise and sell immediately.

If your client plans to sell immediately after exercise but anticipates near-term appreciation in the stock, she will likely want to exercise now and then hold for the minimum one year to get long-term capital gains treatment. Here, again, the minimum future stock price required should be calculated to test the strength of the client's optimism.

If the client has multiple options at different exercise prices, the future stock price that would justify holding for one year to qualify for long-term capital gains will be the same for each option. The smaller future capital gains benefits exactly offset the larger current exercise costs at the same future price, and vice versa. Therefore, if your client is confident that the required future price for *any* option will be achieved, that confidence will justify early exercise of *all* current in-the-money NQSOs. If he's not confident of that price, no justification exists for exercising and then holding any of them. You need to do the calculation only once. For example, if your client has two options, one at $10 and another at $15, to exercise stock selling at $20, the future price one year from the purchase date would have to be the same $21.42 to justify exercising ***and holding*** either one of them. (See ***Figure 3.6***.)

When making all these calculations, it's necessary to assume some discounting or compounding rate. For *diversification* opportunities, the conventional choice in financial analysis is the client's investment opportunity rate. This rate reflects the amount the client

FIGURE 3.6 **Minimum Future Price to Justify Current Exercise and Sale After One Year**

	$10 OPTION		$15 OPTION	
	Exercise Now and Sell	**Exercise Now and Hold One Year**	**Exercise Now and Sell**	**Exercise Now and Hold One Year**
Price at sale	$20.00	**$21.42**	$20.00	**$21.42**
Tax on appreciation	N/A	(0.22)	N/A	(0.22)
Exercise price	(10.00)	(10.00)	(15.00)	(15.00)
Tax on exercise @ 36.45%*	(3.65)	(3.65)	(1.82)	(1.82)
Opportunity return @ 6% after tax	0.38		0.19	
Opportunity cost on exercise and tax		(0.81)		(1.01)
	$6.74	**$6.74**	**$3.37**	**$3.37**

*35% federal tax rate plus 1.45% Medicare rate.

Source: Kochis Fitz

would otherwise be earning, in appropriately risk-adjusted terms, either with the money required in exercise costs and taxes or with the money that could be made available as proceeds of a transaction. Today, for example, a client who would either draw from (to cover costs) or add to (by applying proceeds) a broadly diversified equity portfolio might assume an opportunity rate of, say, 8 or 9 percent pretax total return.

But because of the leverage inherent in options (see "Option Leverage," page 43), the stock under option can, in fact, perform less well than the diversified alternative and still produce equivalent wealth. Consequently, you must help clients recognize that the degrees of risk associated with those calculated returns are not equivalent. A concentrated position carries greater—possibly far greater—risk than an alternative portfolio of broadly diversified investments. The opportunity return expected on that diversified alternative forms the basis for the calculations of the minimum likely performance required of the option alternative (that is, a return your client believes carries virtually no risk). To level the leveraged playing field, we often artificially increase the diversified investment opportunity rate to test the client's confidence as much as possible.

Swapping

If your client decides to exercise an option and hold the acquired stock because he's convinced that future stock growth will more than compensate for the forgone diversified returns and the continued risk of concentration, it's still wise to hedge the bet. Here's how.

Most stock-option plans permit exercise by "swapping" existing long shares in your client's portfolio. These plans permit the option holder to exchange sufficient existing shares to meet the cost of exercise instead of paying cash to cover the cost. Those exchanged shares remain unchanged, keeping their initial acquisition date and basis. A special caution is in order here: shares previously acquired through ISO exercises must be held for the requisite one- and two-year periods before they're eligible to be swapped. Any swap of ISO shares not held long enough would be a disqualifying disposition of those shares.

The incremental, newly acquired shares, in an amount equal to the spread at exercise, take on characteristics according to their NQSO/ ISO status. NQSO shares are fully taxable and have a basis equal to their value at exercise. ISO shares are subject to AMT only and have two bases: zero for regular tax, the value at exercise for AMT.

The main point of a swap exercise, however, is that only those incremental, spread-value shares are added to the portfolio. Since the overarching objective here is to limit the concentration risk, your client should try to minimize the additions to what is already a problem position by buying the least additional shares necessary. Thus, whenever possible, a diversifying client should exercise by swapping existing shares in the portfolio.

However, clients who want to *maximize* exposure to the stock (see chapter 16) should avoid swaps and pay cash (even using borrowed funds) to buy as many shares under option as possible.

Option Leverage

The key economic benefit of stock options is their leverage. Because option holders can purchase the stock at a fixed price for some period of time, they enjoy an advantage not available to other existing or potential shareholders. Others must pay full price when they buy the stock, and they can control the opportunity for further growth in value only by making the investment in the stock's current value. And, of course, they risk losing value in full measure as prices decline from current values. Option holders, instead, will pay a discounted price and can control opportunity for future growth at no out-of-pocket cost, and the value of their opportunity per share can decline only as low as the exercise price.

Option leverage is dynamic. Until the market value first exceeds the option exercise price, the leverage is purely theoretical, but it peaks when the price differential spread first emerges. As the price continues to increase, the leverage diminishes. An option to exercise at $10 for a stock now selling at $10.05 has virtually infinite leverage, whereas the same option for a stock now selling at $1,000 per share has far less. Leverage is not the measure of the current capturable value but of the remaining future potential value—which is far greater with a five-cent current spread than with a spread that has already accumulated $990 of value. The five-cent current spread requires only a .03 percent annual *pretax* stock-growth rate to beat a 6 percent *after-tax* opportunity rate, whereas the $990 spread requires a 5.95 percent growth rate to overcome that opportunity cost. Note that even with that very large current spread, the option can *still* underperform the alternative and produce equivalent results.

Option leverage is also a function of time, diminishing as the option ages. An option with nine years remaining has much more leverage than one with only nine months. In the less extreme case of an option at $10 for a stock selling at $20, when the marginal federal tax rate is 35 percent and the opportunity rate is 6 percent after tax, the required growth rate for the stock is over 4 percent (or almost 5.3 percent annualized) if the expiration is only nine months away. But the rate is only 3.3 percent annualized if the expiration is nine years away. And, of course, on the date the option expires, the leverage declines to nothing. Either your client exercises on that date at that market price or she forfeits that option forever. The opportunity for leverage with that option is past.

Happily, most clients are inclined to exercise options before the spread gets too large (fearing there may be little opportunity left) and before the option gets too old (fearing that the current opportunity may not last over the little time left). Given a choice, almost all clients choose to exercise their oldest, lowest-priced options first. That intuition is correct. And if they're limiting their concentration risk, they want to sell the acquired shares as quickly as they can. So far, so good.

Long Shares: No Leverage

Clients lucky enough to hold stock options probably also own long shares in the same stock, adding to the concentration problem you're trying to help them manage. Like any other shareholder's stock, those long shares have no leverage. That they may have been acquired by exercising options doesn't matter. Their leverage value ended on the date of exercise. Going forward, these shares bear the same benefits or burdens as those owned by any other stockholder.

Ironically, long shares also take on a tax-related characteristic more onerous than that of options. It's helpful to remind yourself and your client why you're entertaining any sale of the company's stock: to minimize the risk that the price will *decline*. If an existing long share declines by $1, the net loss to your client is probably $0.85 per share (assuming that $1 is in excess of the stock's basis and considering only the 15 percent federal tax on long-term capital gain). Every potential share purchasable under option, of course, loses the same nominal $1, but the net cost to your client is probably at most $0.65 per share (assuming an NQSO and the maximum federal tax bracket of 35 percent). Seen in this light, the downside risk is much costlier for long shares than for options.

Ordering Rule

So, both in terms of leveraging any upside potential your client still hopes for and of minimizing the true after-tax costs of the downside potential he rightly fears, he should *plan to sell long shares first* and then exercise and sell NQSOs. Exercising and selling ISOs should come last (whether a year later or right away). In choosing from any of these options, your client should exercise and sell the oldest, lowest-priced options first. Because of their diminishing leverage, these options become more and more like *de*leveraged long shares.

The wisdom of selling long shares first is not intuitive for most clients. It often requires explanation at several points along the way: as you're developing the plan for diversification; when the time comes to take action; and often after the fact, as the second-guessing opportunities emerge, especially if the stock price goes up right after the sale.

The preference clients often have for selling long shares last is another example of the legacy effect. Long shares are somehow more "real" for clients, who often develop a strong sense of loyalty to those shares in return for the financial support they have provided. The value of shares available under option, in contrast, is contingent, merely potential, not yet deserving of respect. Selling them is easy; selling shares already in the portfolio is, for some, almost a betrayal.

Nevertheless, the purity of the theoretically optimal sequencing must sometimes yield to other imperatives. Formal corporate stockholding requirements—or even the unspoken strictures of corporate politics—sometimes intervene. Although either transaction would be reported to the SEC (see chapter 1), in some corporations, exercising options and selling the resulting stock (especially through "cashless" exercise techniques or to cover tax withholding requirements, for example) is a nonevent. The sale of a preexisting stock holding, however, could draw lots of negative attention.

Of course, the advice you give clients on concentrated stock must take the measure of the full context of their circumstances. Nothing is so extraordinary about concentrated stock positions that they should cause you to depart from that most fundamental client-service principle. Understanding the proper ordering of events for optimizing the diversification plan is essential, but the final execution may have to accommodate a variety of client and employer foibles.

4 Diversification Sales and Deferred-Compensation Plans

At first glance, deferred-compensation plans may seem ill suited to the task of managing concentrated stock risk—especially if the plan permits or even requires the deferral to take the form of company stock. Of course, if your client is attempting to maximize opportunity returns through the company stock (see chapter 16), then deferring compensation into company stock without tax on the way in can be an exceptionally efficient technique. But if, instead, your client is trying to reduce exposure to that stock's risks, the last thing he should do is buy more of it.

Obviously, it would be better to reduce exposure by using the deferred-compensation plan for other diversification opportunities. Using fixed-income return deferral choices to fulfill fixed-income allocation targets within the client's total portfolio could maximize the deferred-compensation plan's investment advantage. But using the deferred-compensation plan to add high equity returns to the total mix could be even better. If your clients could get the proceeds from selling concentrated stock or exercising options into plans like these—to take advantage of those preferred returns—it would be so much easier to overcome the barriers to sale because subsequent opportunities could be so much more attractive.

Well, they can get those proceeds in, albeit indirectly.

I am unaware of any deferred-compensation plans that permit the direct, tax-free deferral of outright sales of long shares. I doubt the tax law could be outmaneuvered to permit that; however, I know of some deferred-compensation plans that directly permit the tax-free deferral of stock-option exercises. Here the tax maneuvering is, though complex, still possible. For example, a stock-option plan could provide for automatic exercises at particular prices or times and permit option holders to defer in advance the income, if any, that would otherwise occur. But *every* deferred-compensation plan permits the *indirect* deferral of option or long-share sale proceeds.

For a better understanding of how that's done and why it presents such an attractive opportunity to manage concentration risk, let's look first at the evolution of deferred-compensation plans.

Deferred Compensation: Then and Now

When I began practicing financial planning in the early 1970s, a marginal income tax rate of 90 percent was a relatively recent memory. Tax liberalization reduced that marginal rate to a mere 70 percent on investment income, with a maximum rate on current compensation of 50 percent, but the seeds of tax-rate arbitrage through compensation deferral had already been sown.

At first, deferred-compensation plans provided only for deferral itself: "Don't pay me now when I'll be taxed at 90 percent; pay me later when I'm retired and in a lower tax bracket." In those days, the brackets were so steeply graduated—and the absolute amounts of executive compensation and retirement benefits so much smaller than they are today—that even the most senior executives could expect to be in lower brackets once they retired. Today, the brackets are so compressed and executive compensation levels so high that no pre- to post-employment tax-rate arbitrage is expected. All analysis is now done at the same, highest marginal rate. That was not always the case.

For a short time after its installation, the 50 percent maximum tax on compensation income applied only to *current* employment income (and to retirement income but only for the first year after employment ended). Subsequent retirement income was taxed at the normal rates, which ran as high as 70 percent. These rules could turn a deferral of compensation into a disaster: income that would be taxed at no more than 50 percent might be deferred to a time when it could be taxed at a rate as high as 70 percent. Something had to be done. It was.

Sweetening the Pot

Deferred-compensation plans began providing for an added benefit: the deferred amounts would earn some rate of return. Once this return feature was introduced, it continued as part of the plans, even after the 50 percent maximum tax rate was extended to cover all post-employment retirement benefits as well. As a result, the worst fate for deferred-compensation was for it to be taxed later at a rate of 50 percent, the same rate that would have applied now had it not been deferred.

The interim-return feature, not tax-rate arbitrage, became the main event in deferred-compensation plans—and it was quite a performance. At first, deferred-compensation-plan returns were fairly tame, promising earnings tied to some relatively low-risk, fixed-income return rate like the prime rate or short-term Treasury instruments. To improve on those results, some companies added a premium to the base rate (prime rate plus 2 percent, for example) or chose a measure reflecting much longer-term or lower-quality securities. Since the late 1980s, equity-return measures, with their greater investment risks—and greater return potential—have become commonplace. Some employers now even permit plan participants, in effect, to choose from several investment-return options and modify those choices over time. As a result, for many executives, deferred-compensation plans have become an integral, if somewhat cumbersome, part of their investment portfolio, requiring careful coordination as part of the overall investment plan.

The investment value of the opportunity to defer compensation is difficult to overstate. Like qualified deferred-contribution plans, such as 401(k) and Keogh plans, the amounts deferred (contributed) are free of tax at the outset and can grow on a tax-deferred basis until distribution. What's more, unlike qualified plans, no legal limits apply to how much may be deposited in a deferred-compensation plan. The American Jobs Creation Act of 2004 imposed new requirements on the timing of deferral elections and distributions and restricted the ability to change those distribution decisions, but it imposed no limits on the *size* of the deferral. Plans therefore commonly provide that 100 percent of any bonuses and 50 percent of salary—sometimes even more—may be contributed. Clearly, the amounts going into the plans can be very large, indeed, and the corresponding investment opportunities can become a central component of many executives' total investment portfolios.

Risks and Returns

You should find it helpful, as will most of your clients, to focus first on the return potential of deferred-compensation plans. Put simply, the deferral of tax, all other things being equal, transforms a pretax return into an after-tax return. An equity-based total pretax return of, say, 9 percent, becomes, in effect, a 9 percent *after-tax* return when achieved in a deferred-compensation plan. (See ***Figure 4.1***.)

Needless to say, a 9 percent *pretax* return can be achieved with much less risk than a 9 percent *after-tax* return. Even if fully eligible for 15 percent long-term capital gains tax or 15 percent dividend treatment, a pretax return of 10.6 percent would be required to net a 9 percent after-tax return. If that 10.6 percent pretax return could be achieved in a deferred-compensation plan, the *after-tax* equivalent for the nondeferral alternative would have to be 10.6 percent. All other things being equal, the deferred-compensation plan always wins when the pretax-return choices within the plan are equivalent to those outside of it. But all other things are not always equal.

The strong return advantage of deferred-compensation plans comes at significant costs—both actual and potential. One fundamental constraint is that your client must make the decision to defer income before she has a right to receive it. A core, long-standing doctrine of U.S. tax law is that of constructive receipt. If you're entitled to receive income, declining voluntarily to do so does not shelter that income from tax. You're required to pay tax on income you could receive—even if you choose not to. Consequently, to defer tax liabil-

FIGURE 4.1 **After-Tax Equivalent Returns**

$100,000 Compensation	**Deferred**	**Not Deferred**
Gross initial amount	$100,000	$100,000
Current tax (35%)	N/A	(35,000)
Net investable amount	100,000	65,000
Deferred for 10 years @ 9% **pretax** return	237,000	
Invested for 10 years @ 9% **after-tax** return		154,000
Tax on receipt (35%)	(83,000)	Included in assumed net **after-tax** return)
Net value in 10 years	$154,000	$154,000

Source: Kochis Fitz

ity on deferred compensation, the decision to defer the income must be irrevocable and must be made before you're entitled to receive it.

The IRS has long interpreted this timing requirement to mean that the decision to defer must be made in the tax year *before* the year in which the income would have been earned. That means the decision to defer must be made in year one on salary to be paid in year two. The same would apply to a bonus for year two even if it were not to be paid until year three. Over the years, the courts have generally disagreed with these restrictions and have permitted a more liberal use of deferral. Some deferred-compensation plans have permitted deferral elections of bonuses, for example, right up to the point of decision about whether and how much bonus will be paid. However, with some exceptions for newly eligible plan participants and with transition rules still to be developed, the American Jobs Creation Act of 2004 statutorily resolved this issue in favor of the IRS position, requiring deferral elections in the year *before* the compensation is earned.

In any event, regardless of the timing of the election, the irrevocability of that election is a somewhat loose concept. In recent years, many deferred-compensation plans had permitted participants to reconsider their decisions. In effect, plans permitted participants to change their original deferral decision, generally to receive the deferred funds sooner or later than originally planned. The 2004 legislation continues to permit such "second looks" but permits changes only to make the actual payments *later* than originally elected. In our view, the new law will accomplish little in constraining potential abuse of the constructive-receipt rule. It will merely encourage participants to make very short-term initial deferral elections and later, as each distribution point approaches, extend the distribution into the future if that then serves their purposes.

Still, for most executives, these constraints on deferral timing and payout flexibility are modest compared with the perceived risks of higher future taxes and actual financial jeopardy to the funds while deferred. Now more than ever, with ordinary income tax rates as low as most people can recall, many are inclined to believe that rates will rise to fund governmental functions and programs and to combat fiscal deficits. And that leads quite a few executives to fear that deferring compensation may amount to moving income out of a low tax-rate environment and into one with higher rates.

It's an important concern, but advisers can readily provide clients with valuable guidance. Depending on the expected return rates inside and outside the deferred-compensation plan and the anticipated deferral period, you can calculate precisely how much higher those future tax rates would have to be to counteract the benefits of deferral. In our experience, most clients quickly dismiss this fear of higher tax rates once they see results like those shown in ***Figure 4.2***. The figure shows the ***minimum*** future federal tax rate required, assuming a current rate of 35 percent and an after-tax opportunity rate for nondeferred funds of only 4 percent after tax.

If your client thinks that modest rate increases are likely, is not optimistic about achieving a greater pretax return in the plan than the likely after-tax return outside of it, and plans to defer only for a relatively short time, then deferral is unwise. Most clients, however,

FIGURE 4.2 **Minimum Future Tax Rates**

	Rate of Return (Pretax) in Deferred-Compensation Plan		
Deferral Period	**5%**	**7.5%**	**10%**
3 years	37%	41%	45%
5 years	38	45	51
10 years	41	53	63

Source: Kochis Fitz

are optimistic about the return advantage and plan relatively long deferrals, so they usually overcome fears that tax rates will rise much higher. They can therefore proceed to consider the other big worry: will the money deferred actually be there when the time comes?

A decision to defer income is a decision to substitute assured money now for a promise from the employer to pay later instead. To meet tax-law requirements, no dollars may be set aside to specifically fund the individual executive's deferred-compensation account. The deferred-compensation promise is simply an unsecured contractual obligation of the employer, no better than the claims of any other unsecured creditor and inferior to the claims of those creditors with security rights against the employer's assets.

Nevertheless, actual funds may be earmarked, in fact, to provide resources to cover these obligations, and the deferring executive may even be given a great deal of influence over how those earmarked funds are to be invested in the interim. Still, up to the point at which the deferred compensation is actually paid, it is subject to the risk of the employer's insolvency.

In our experience, most executives are very optimistic that their employer will continue to have the wherewithal to make good on these promises. That's generally the case even over very long deferral periods and even when the payment is scheduled to be made many years after the executives have left the company (and are therefore no longer able to assess its strengths from an inside perspective). Still, others consider the risks of the employer's eventual insolvency to be more than just theoretical and consequently decide to pass on deferral.

But even if your client resolves his concerns about higher tax rates or about the employer's insolvency, there is still another potential trap: the possibility of the employer's *unwillingness* to pay, regardless of its ability to do so. Such recalcitrance risk is not widely feared among the rank and file of eligible deferred-compensation participants, but it's occasionally a serious concern among very senior executives. They are the people most likely to be dismissed if control of the company changes hands, especially on unfriendly terms. New management and a new board won't necessarily treat the displaced senior management team quite so generously. Deliberate foot dragging and administrative barriers could arise, perhaps even forcing the former executives to resort to the costs and risks of litigation to combat the company's hopes of getting them to settle for less than 100 cents on the dollar.

The Rabbi Trust

The now-famous rabbi trust is a device designed to address the risk that employers may hold back deferred-compensation entitlements. Some years ago, a rabbi was negotiating a compensation package with the leaders of his congregation. Some of his total compensation was to be deferred to a later date, but the rabbi was concerned that the congregation might later renege on its promise if it wasn't satisfied with his services while he was actively employed. The solution was to put the funds needed to pay the deferred compensation into a third-party trust that would make the payments as scheduled when the payments were due, regardless of the gratitude or chagrin of the congregation. To avoid the constructive-receipt problem, the assets in that rabbi trust were at all times subject to the claims of the congregation's general creditors.

Today, many deferred-compensation arrangements are funded with assets placed in a rabbi trust in order to make good on the employer's promises at the scheduled times, whether or not the employer is eager to make them. Some of the more conservative deferred-compensation plans were even structured with rabbi trusts housed overseas in jurisdictions that make it notoriously difficult to tamper with the original trust terms and with overseas trust companies that are less likely to adhere to the wishes of the current management of a U.S. company. In all events, however, whether domestic or overseas, any rabbi-trust assets were required to be subject to the claims of the employer's general creditors. The 2004 American Jobs Creation Act now precludes the use of an offshore trust.

Investment Options

Often, the investment opportunities available within a company's deferred-compensation plan are comparable to the choices available in that company's qualified plans—for example, its 401(k) plan. The wisdom of this arrangement is, of course, debatable, but it could have at least one potentially harmful outcome. Many 401(k) plans provide investment in the employer's stock as an available, even favored, alternative. Some provide matching contributions only in the form of company stock. The fate of Enron stock and other recent failures demonstrate the potentially devastating impact of this 401(k) feature on the financial health of employees of small or moderate means. Having deferred-compensation plans also adopt employer stock as an available, or even preferred, alternative brings this potential for pain to the more well-to-do employee ranks as an ironically symmetrical, if unintended, consequence.

And this brings us full circle, to the goal of getting the proceeds of concentrated stock sales or options exercises into deferred-compensation plans to achieve diversification and to take advantage of the exceptionally strong after-tax-equivalent returns of deferred-compensation plans.

The Benefits of Deferral

One of the fundamental truisms of all financial planning is that the only thing anyone can spend is *cash*. It doesn't really matter where that cash comes from: dividends, interest, proceeds of sales of assets, or paychecks. While employed, everyone, from the most senior executives on down, is accustomed to covering ordinary living expenses from salary, perhaps drawing a little—or a lot—more from bonus payments. But there's no special advantage to funding one's cost of living that way; exercising a stock option and selling the stock acquired can produce equivalent cash and at no worse tax exposure. Sale of long shares within a concentrated stock position can do even better, producing cash at capital gains tax rates only on the gain portion.

The cash produced by any such long-share sales or option exercises and sales frees up as much or more cash available to be deferred from salary and bonus. For example, even if long shares had a zero basis, at the 15 percent federal capital gains tax, sales of $100,000 worth of a concentrated position would produce $85,000 of spendable cash. To net that much cash from salary at a 35 percent tax rate, the pretax salary would need to be nearly $131,000.

This available tax leverage can make the indirect compensation-deferral technique a very attractive method of managing a concentrated stock position. As the example illustrates, $100,000 from the concentrated stock position could produce $131,000 from other sources to be invested elsewhere. With any basis in that concentrated position, the leverage gets even better. But that's not the only benefit. That compensation, once deferred, enjoys the preferential return opportunities of the deferred-compensation shelter, turning pretax returns into after-tax returns. That's tantamount to selling long shares, for example, at no tax and putting the proceeds to work at after-tax rates.

This indirect deferral strategy has another, very significant benefit: the imperative to fund living expenses. Remember, deferred-compensation decisions have to be made in advance and are irrevocable, at least in the short term. The salary or bonus compensation is gone; the expenses remain. Having deferred the otherwise available cash from compensation, your client will be forced to sell *something*. The best candidate, of course, is the risky, concentrated stock position.

In more than a few cases, we've seen this advance commitment's spending imperative provide the discipline necessary to actually get the concentrated stock sold. One of our clients long ago embarked on a plan to defer compensation each year and then to sell sufficient shares each year to replace the absent cash. Each year, in the spring, we struggle through this client's pangs of regret as he sells shares, grudgingly, but necessarily, to meet living expenses, and late each fall, he steels himself to once again defer, knowing what's soon to come. The consolation for this client is the requirement in his company's deferred-compensation plan that at least 20 percent of the deferral be invested in company stock. Still, 80 percent diversification is better than none.

The Coin's Two Sides

Deferred-compensation plans have some peculiar risks and limitations. Offsetting their investment advantage are the interim illiquidity they impose and the uncertainty of the employer's future ability and willingness to pay the amounts deferred. If your client's concentrated stock position is in employer stock—the likely case for a client who has a deferred-compensation arrangement—the use of a deferred-compensation plan as a diversification device has one considerable advantage and one clear disadvantage. The benefit, of course, is the ability to indirectly translate the concentrated position into a broadly diversified alternative investment with the potential for high returns. The drawback is that that transformation relies on the success of the same company for the eventual availability of spendable results. *Equity* risk in Company X is exchanged for *credit* risk in Company X. These risks are not identical, of course, but they're related and tend to move in the same direction. A weak stock price could easily coincide with a company's ample ability to fund contractual obligations. But a company unable to meet contractual obligations is unlikely to enjoy a robust stock price.

So, using a deferred-compensation plan as a strategy to minimize the risk of a concentrated stock position moves the downside protection a theoretical notch higher, from equity status to creditor status, with the added potential benefit of improved investment performance along the way. These advantages must be weighed against the risks of the employer's future inability or unwillingness to pay. Some clients are just not willing to bear those risks, even with the promise of preferred investment performance. For them, deferred-compensation strategies are no solution to concentration problems. But most clients dismiss their employer's creditor risks as inconsequential. They are likely to be the most optimistic about the stock's future price potential. Ironically, therefore, they make the best candidates for this diversification strategy.

Quite a few clients are in the middle ground: reasonably optimistic about the concentrated stock's price potential and not overly skeptical of the company's future ability and willingness to make good on the deferred-compensation contract. For them, the key motivator is the opportunity for improved returns within the deferred-compensation plan. For them, an indirect deferral, therefore, often constitutes an important *part* of their overall diversification strategy.

5 An Out for Insiders

Directors and senior executives of public companies often own very large concentrations of the stock of the companies on whose boards they serve or the companies they work for. Such ownership is burdened with strict limitations on the freedom to sell shares of that stock. These restrictions can create severe investment risk. Opportunities for career advancement, formal shareholding minimums, and the expectations of financial analysts—not to mention the expectations of shareholders—each erect barriers to the sale of company stock. But perhaps most significant are the federal law (SEC Rule 10b5) and the many state laws that prohibit trading on *material inside information*—that is, information not available to the public and likely to affect the stock price. Unfortunately, directors and senior corporate executives can find themselves in a position to have access to such information at almost any time, putting almost any sale of stock into a gray area perilously close to illegality. Most companies have attempted to alleviate the problem by establishing (usually brief) trading windows four times a year, shortly after reporting quarterly results, during which transactions should be safe.

In 2000, the SEC adopted a rule that produced an even better solution to help corporate executives and directors develop less-risky investment strategies for concentrated stock. This rule created an important opportunity for greater flexibility and greater safety both in pursuing appropriate investment diversification and in accomplishing specific financial objectives.

SEC Rule 10b5-1 Plans

The rule adopted by the SEC in 2000 established that *prearranged* plans for stock sales—called Rule 10b5-1 plans—may constitute a defense against a claim of violation of the federal inside-information prohibition—regardless of when the sale occurs and even if inside information, in fact, is known to the seller when the sale occurs.

Several key requirements apply to these plans:

♦ The contract, instructions, or written plan must be established *before* the executive/director becomes aware of the material inside information.

♦ The contract, instructions, or plan must either (a) specify the amount, price, and date; or (b) provide a written formula for determining those parameters—for example, "On the first market day of each quarter, sell 2,000 shares of XYZ stock as long as the sales price equals or exceeds $30 per share"—and not permit any subsequent discretion by the executive over how, when, or whether to execute the plan.

♦ The executive/director does not enter into or alter a corresponding or hedging position regarding the same stock (see chapter 15).

♦ Although the SEC doesn't require this, many corporations insist that any 10b5-1 plans for their officers and directors be adopted only during trading windows.

Essentially, the prearranged-sale plan is either on automatic pilot or it's not; your clients can't have it both ways. Moreover, they can't abandon the plan and still expect this defense to work. In fact, the more a client modifies or interrupts a 10b5-1 plan, the more susceptible it is to claims of inside-information trading. Once a plan is in place, it's generally a bad idea to undertake any other transaction in the company stock. After all, if the defense of 10b5-1 was intended to cover valid diversification strategies, why wasn't that particular transaction made part of the plan?

Although a prearranged-sale plan can solve some problems, it can create others. What seems like a good idea at one point could become a straitjacket later, and getting out of that straitjacket can make a new plan, or the absence of a plan, more suspect. Consequently, the best way to handle the client's desire to take a second look is to assign any 10b5-1 plan only a brief duration—say, one year at most—with the expectation of creating a new plan at that juncture to replace the expiring plan. What's more, the terms of the plan itself might include a termination provision for certain events such as the company's merger or acquisition, the client's divorce, or the onset of a serious illness.

Third-Party Discretion

Rather than using a prearranged plan as a defense, the executive/director may delegate all trading discretion to a third party who is not in possession of inside information. This choice is not yet popular because such delegation is fraught with client-satisfaction risks and endless opportunities for second-guessing the third party's decisions.

Formula Plans

Instead of accepting discretion, most advisers help their clients develop gradual, automatic diversification strategies that may cover different amounts of shares at different times and different prices and which can be related to the stock's price performance relative to some benchmark. An advance formula's capacity to approximate what would be the parameters of the client's own discretionary decisions is limited only by the adviser's creativity. An example of an actual 10b5-1 plan, designed to get very close to what the client *would* do if he could, is set out in the appendix to this chapter on page 64.

Indeed, advisers are helping clients devise sophisticated sales programs—to be executed automatically—to accomplish specific financial goals in specified amounts and at specified times. For example, a 10b5-1 plan targeted to cover the costs of an anticipated home purchase, with a backup provision to achieve some investment diversification could look something like this: "On the first market day of September 20xx, sell sufficient shares of ISO-acquired stock to qualify for long-term capital gain treatment and generate pretax proceeds equal to 125 percent of the purchase price of a residential property I may purchase between now and that date, but in no event less than $1 million or more than $2 million. If I have made no such purchase, sell only 10,000 shares at a price no less than $25 per share."

Short-Swing Constraints

For directors and insider executives subject to the special Rule 16b restrictions on purchases and sales of stock within six months, 10b5-1 plans provide no additional benefit. It merely helps keep a sale from being considered a violation of actual inside-information constraints. It doesn't do anything to address the problem of purchases made within six months before or after the sales. Remember, however, that under appropriate corporate plans, exercising an option isn't considered a purchase. So a 10b5-1 plan could specify: "For the nonqualified stock option granted in August 20xx: On the first business day of January 20xx, exercise options and immediately sell resulting shares sufficient to generate at least $500,000 in pretax, net proceeds."

Sales During Retirement-Plan Blackout Periods

In contrast, 10b5-1 plans do help with the problem of trying to sell during the prohibited blackout periods for the company's retirement plans. The Sarbanes-Oxley prohibition against sales during retirement-plan blackout periods specifically exempts sales that occur under 10b5-1 plans.

Plan Logistics

To maximize the benefits of the 10b5-1 plan, some degree of public disclosure is wise. There is no need to reveal the details of the plan, but the fact that there *is* a plan can be disclosed on SEC Form 8-K. Very prominent corporate leaders might even want to issue a press release. The corporation's legal office and public relations or shareholder relations departments will be helpful in these areas.

Following that disclosure, it's usually best to delay any actual transaction until any potentially adverse publicity has subsided. The plan might have an effective date, say, thirty or forty-five days after the date of publication. When transactions under the plan do occur, the SEC disclosure filings should identify that they occurred pursuant to a 10b5-1 plan. Observers of insider stock sales will know it's not the result of an ad hoc, discretionary decision but instead is the outcome of a previously adopted plan.

Prearranged Plans: A Corporate Requirement?

Although these planning arrangements came into use only in 2000, it's likely that many companies will eventually make the adoption of 10b5-1 plans a requirement for their senior executives and directors. The broad availability of this defense, regardless of window periods, could appeal greatly to many public corporations eager to minimize corporate embarrassment or actual liability for the actions of their senior people.

Personal financial advisers will, of course, welcome this requirement because it will reinforce employer support for the legitimacy of diversification and will remove one of the more powerful constraints against it. "The SEC won't let me diversify!" will no longer be a valid excuse.

Appendix

XYZ Co. Nondiscretionary Rule 10b5-1 Sales Plan

This sales plan ("Sales Plan"), dated May 9, 2004 (the "Adoption Date"), is between Client ("Seller") and Adviser ("Investment Manager").

WHEREAS, Seller currently has in place an XYZ Co. nondiscretionary Rule 10b5-1 sales plan dated May 21, 2002 (the "Existing Plan"), which Seller desires to terminate effective as of April 1, 2004; and

WHEREAS, Seller desires to establish this Sales Plan as of the Adoption Date to exercise the nonqualified stock options in grants number 012345, 012346, 012347, and 012348 and sell the resulting shares of common stock of XYZ Co. ("Issuer"), with such sales of shares to begin not earlier than the Effective Time (as defined below); and

WHEREAS, Seller desires that this Sales Plan comply with the requirements of Rule 10b5-1(c)(1) under the Securities Exchange Act of 1934, as amended; and

WHEREAS, Seller desires to engage Investment Manager through a broker of its choice to effect sales of shares of Issuer's stock (the "Shares") in accordance with the Sales Plan;

NOW, THEREFORE, Seller and Investment Manager hereby agree as follows:

1 Sales Terms

(a) General. This plan provides for the exercise of the then remaining nonqualified stock options in grants 012345, 012346, 012347, and 012348, and the sale of the resulting Shares. The options in grant 012345 are to be exercised and sold first. After all options in that grant have been sold, the options in grant 012346 are to be exercised and sold, followed by those in grant 012347, then those in grant 012348. Such sales shall not commence until the first trading day that occurs after ninety days have elapsed since

the Adoption Date (such time, the "Effective Time"). Thereafter, sales will occur weekly, subject to the closing-price requirements set forth below and to any suspension of trading as set forth in section 3 below (a "Suspension"), during which time they shall cease until such Suspension has terminated. The number of Shares sold each week will depend on the closing market price of the stock on the last trading day of the week immediately preceding the week in which the sales are to take place according to the terms hereof (the "Reference Date"). An applicable stock closing price will be determined on the Reference Date for each week that this Sales Plan is in place, and the number of Shares to be sold during the week subsequent to the applicable Reference Date ("Applicable Share Number"), except in the event of a Suspension, during which no sales will take place, will be determined by reference to the table below.

Stock Closing Price on the Reference Date	Applicable Share Number
Below $20.00	10,000
$20.00–$30.00	15,000
$30.01–$40.00	20,000
Above $40.00	25,000

Source: Kochis Fitz

Upon determining that Shares are to be sold in accordance with the provisions of this paragraph (a) during the week following a Reference Date, Investment Manager shall promptly notify Issuer of the Applicable Share Number. During the calendar week subsequent to the applicable Reference Date, Investment Manager shall use its best efforts to sell a number of shares which totals the Applicable Share Number at such time or times as it determines in its sole discretion. Immediately prior to each sale, Investment Manager shall notify Issuer's stock administrator ("Stock Administrator") and general counsel ("General Counsel") so that procedures for exercise of options for the number of Shares to be sold can be effected. In the event that the Applicable Share Number is not sold during the calendar week following the Reference Date, any Shares not sold shall not be carried over to the subsequent week.

(b) Remaining Shares in Grant 012346. In the event that not all the shares in option grant 012346 have been exercised and sold prior to the earnings release for Issuer's fourth quarter of fiscal 2006, then during the week beginning on the day that occurs after two full trading days have elapsed since the earnings release for Issuer's fourth quarter of fiscal 2006, all remaining options in grant 012346 shall be exercised and sold at market. Immediately prior to such sale, Investment Manager shall notify Issuer's Stock Administrator and General Counsel so that procedures for exercise of options for the number of Shares to be sold can be effected.

All option exercises made in connection with the sales of Shares under this Sales Plan shall require payment by Seller to Issuer of such consideration as may be required to comply with Section 402(a) of the Sarbanes-Oxley Act of 2002.

2 Term and Expiration. This Sales Plan shall expire on the earliest of

(a) August 1, 2007;

(b) the public announcement of the execution of a definitive agreement or plan relating to (i) the liquidation or dissolution of Issuer; (ii) the sale of all or substantially all of Issuer's assets to an unrelated party; or (iii) a merger, reorganization, consolidation, or other transaction if the holders of Issuer's outstanding voting power immediately prior to such transaction do not own a majority of the outstanding voting power of Issuer or the successor entity immediately upon completion of the transaction; and

(c) the sale of all the Shares according to the terms hereof.

3 Suspensions

(a) Affecting Investment Manager. Seller understands that, despite Investment Manager's best efforts to effect a sale in accordance with this agreement, Investment Manager may not be able to effect such a sale due to a market disruption or a legal, regulatory, or contractual

restriction applicable to Investment Manager or any other event or circumstance beyond Investment Manager's control in its exercise of reasonable diligence (an "Investment Manager Suspension"). Seller also understands that even in the absence of an Investment Manager Suspension, Investment Manager may be unable to effect sales consistent with ordinary principles of best execution due to insufficient volume of trading, failure of the stock to reach and sustain a limit order price, or other market factors in effect on the date of a sale ("Unfilled Sales").

(b) Affecting Seller. None of (i) a previously unscheduled or special blackout period that is not a Suspension, (ii) a general prohibition on insider trading due to possession of material inside information regarding Issuer, or (iii) the quarterly blackout period under the XYZ Co. statement of policy against insider trading shall affect the operation of this Sales Plan. However, Investment Manager agrees that if Issuer enters into a transaction that results in the imposition of trading restrictions on Seller, such as a stock offering requiring an affiliate lockup, or due to any other legal, regulatory, or contractual restriction on Seller (other than Seller's possession of material inside information regarding the Issuer) (a "Special Issuer Suspension"), then Investment Manager will cease effecting sales under this Sales Plan as soon as written notice signed by the compliance officer under Issuer's statement of policy against insider trading of such Special Issuer Suspension is actually received, until notified in writing by such compliance officer that such Special Issuer Suspension has terminated. Notice will be considered received when Investment Manager acknowledges receipt. The compliance officer may solicit acknowledgement via a telephone conversation (415/123-4567) with John Advisor or Carol Advisor, or by e-mail (Info@Advisers.com) or fax (415/123-4567). Investment Manager shall resume effecting sales in accordance with this Sales Plan as soon as practicable after the cessation or termination of any Suspension.

(c) Any Unfilled Sales resulting from a Suspension shall be executed as soon as practicable on succeeding trading days, provided, however, in no event shall such Unfilled Sales of Shares take

place under this Sales Plan after the end of the week following the Reference Date.

4 Seller Representations and Warranties. Seller represents and warrants that:

(a) As of the Adoption Date, Seller is not aware of material, non-public information with respect to Issuer or any securities of Issuer (including the Shares); is not subject to any legal, regulatory, or contractual restriction or undertaking that would prevent Investment Manager from conducting sales in accordance with this Sales Plan; and is entering into this Sales Plan in good faith and not as part of a plan or scheme to evade the prohibitions of Rule 10b5-1. Seller shall immediately notify Investment Manager if Seller becomes subject to a legal, regulatory, or contractual restriction or undertaking that would prevent Investment Manager from making sales pursuant to this Sales Plan, and, in such a case, to the extent necessary and appropriate, Seller and Investment Manager shall cooperate to amend or otherwise revise this Sales Plan to take account of such legal, regulatory, or contractual restriction or undertaking (provided that neither party shall be obligated to take any action that would be inconsistent with the requirements of Rule10b5-1(c)).

(b) The Shares are not subject to any liens, encumbrances, security interests, or other impediments to transfer (other than limitations imposed by securities laws).

5 No Subsequent Influence or Control. Seller acknowledges and agrees that she does not have authority, influence, or control over any sales of Shares effected by Investment Manager pursuant to this Sales Plan, and will not attempt to exercise any authority, influence, or control over such sales or provide any material nonpublic information to Investment Manager. Investment Manager agrees not to seek advice from Seller with respect to the manner in which it effects sales under this Sales Plan. During the term of this Sales Plan, Investment Manager agrees that it will not execute any trades in XYZ Co. securities by Seller other than those contemplated hereunder, it being understood that exercising and holding an option shall not constitute a trade.

6 Stock Splits, Combinations, etc., Affecting Stock. The terms of any sales remaining under this Sales Plan under section 1 shall be appropriately adjusted to reflect any stock split, subdivision, combination, reclassification, or similar event affecting the Shares (unless such action results in the termination of this Sales Plan under section 2 above).

7 Intent to Comply With Rule 10b5-1. It is the intent of the parties that this Sales Plan comply with the requirements of Rule 10b5-1(c)(1)(i)(B) under the Securities Exchange Act of 1934 and this Sales Plan shall be interpreted to comply with the requirements of Rule 10b5-1(c).

8 Rule 144 Compliance. Seller is an "affiliate," as that term is used in Rule 144 of the Securities Act of 1933, as amended. Accordingly:

(a) Seller represents and warrants that the Shares to be sold pursuant to this Sales Plan are currently eligible for sale under Rule 144 or 145.

(b) Seller agrees not to take, and agrees to cause any person or entity with which Seller would be required to aggregate sales of Shares pursuant to paragraph (a)(2) or (e) of Rule 144 not to take, any action that would cause the sales hereunder not to meet all applicable requirements of Rule 144.

(c) Seller agrees to complete, execute, and deliver to Investment Manager Forms 144 for the sales to be effected under this Sales Plan at such times and in such numbers as Investment Manager shall request, and Investment Manager agrees to cause a broker selected by it to file such Forms 144 on behalf of Seller as required by applicable law. The "Remarks" section of each Form 144 shall bear a notification stating that the Shares covered by such Form 144 are being sold pursuant to this Sales Plan and that the representation regarding Seller's knowledge of material nonpublic information speaks as of the date that Seller adopted this Sales Plan. If the Shares hereunder are to be sold pursuant to Rule 144 or 145 of the Securities Act, Seller agrees that Investment Manager shall continue making Form

144 filings as contemplated by this subparagraph in connection with sales under this Sales Plan until Investment Manager receives a written notification (which notification shall be acknowledged by Issuer) stating that Seller is no longer an "affiliate" of the Issuer as that term is defined under Rule 144.

(d) Seller hereby grants Investment Manager and/or a broker selected by Investment Manager a power of attorney to complete or file on behalf of Seller any required Forms 144. Notwithstanding such power of attorney, Seller acknowledges that Investment Manager shall have no obligation to complete or file Forms 144 on behalf of Seller except as set forth in subparagraph (c) above.

(e) Investment Manager agrees to conduct all sales pursuant to this Sales Plan in accordance with the manner of sale and current public information requirements of Rule 144 and in no event shall Investment Manager effect any sale if such sale would exceed the then-applicable amount limitation under Rule 144, assuming Investment Manager's sales pursuant to this Sales Plan are the only sales subject to that limitation.

9 Section 13/16 Compliance. Seller agrees to make all filings, if any are required under Sections 13 and 16 of the Exchange Act. Investment Manager shall provide Seller promptly with information regarding all sales so that Seller may make any required Form 4 and other filings on a timely basis, together with specific confirmed notice on the date of sale to Issuer's General Counsel, including the number of Shares sold and their sale price. Each such filing shall indicate by footnote that it took place pursuant to a plan established under Rule 10b5-1.

10 Prohibition of Hedging Transactions. Seller agrees that she will not engage in offsetting or hedging transactions in violation of Rule 10b5-1.

11 Termination of Existing Plan. The Existing Plan, as defined above, shall be terminated and thereafter null and void, as of April 1, 2004.

12 Governing Law, Amendments, and Termination. This Sales Plan shall be governed by and construed in accordance with the laws of the State of California. This Sales Plan may be modified, terminated, or amended only in writing, signed by the parties hereto, and provided that in the case of any modification or amendment, such modification or amendment shall only be permitted at a time when Seller is otherwise permitted to effect sales under Issuer's trading policies, and shall only be permitted at a time when Seller is not aware of material nonpublic information concerning Issuer or its securities.

IN WITNESS WHEREOF, the undersigned have signed this Sales Plan as of May 9, 2004.

SELLER:

____

Client
c/o XYZ Co, Inc.
1 Market Street
Anytown, CA 00100

INVESTMENT MANAGER:

____

John Adviser
AdvisersInc.

6 Restricted Stock: Tackling Temptation

Selling the concentrated stock is usually the first and simplest line of attack in managing the risk of concentrated stock positions. The mirror strategy, of course, is not to buy more of it. That approach is straightforward enough on its face, but for senior executives, the acquisition of company stock seems to have a momentum all its own. Acquisitions stream from many directions: retirement-plan matching contributions in the form of company stock, annual grants of stock options, and, increasingly, grants of restricted shares of company stock. Any one of these channels may necessitate taking aggressive steps to avoid worsening an existing concentration problem. Of the three, restricted stock is the most likely to seduce your client to be unfaithful to the diversification strategy you've devised.

Restricted stock as a compensation device has a long history. For many decades employers have maintained plans under which employees are granted shares of the company stock subject to restrictions that will lapse, if at all, only after the passage of a set amount of time (typically three or five years of service or until normal retirement) or upon achieving some corporate or individual performance goal. Once that time has passed or the goal is accomplished, the restrictions lapse and the restricted stock becomes the property of the employee.

Especially because of concerns about the structural flaws and potential abuses of stock options, restricted stock is enjoying a new popularity. Microsoft, surely the icon of the stock-option culture, announced in 2003 that it would no longer grant stock options but instead use restricted stock as a compensation tool. This impresses me as an extreme example of the general overreaction to the stock-option problems that resulted from the market exuberance of the late 1990s. I won't be surprised if Microsoft reverses itself as market recoveries cause its employees to yearn once again for the leverage that only stock options can provide. Share for share, restricted stock is no match for the wealth-building power of stock options in a rising market.

Managing the Section 83(b) Election

If your client is granted restricted stock, it's critical to review with him the benefits and dangers of Section 83(b), a provision of the Internal Revenue Code. The provision permits an election to treat the property received as compensation (employee stock, for example) as currently taxable income even when that property may subsequently be forfeited. This election must be filed with the IRS within thirty days of initially receiving the restricted stock. IRS regulations—Sections 1.83-2(b), (c), and (d)—specify the information to be included with that election, and the example in the appendix to this chapter illustrates the standard content for the election. This information must also be provided to the employer and attached to the tax return for the year of election.

Normally, the tax liability on restricted stock wouldn't be incurred until the forfeiture risk had lapsed. The payoff for accepting that risk and volunteering to pay tax—not only *early* but also in the face of the possibility that the tax might never be imposed—is the prospect of turning the interim growth in the value of that stock into capital gain and postponing that tax until the stock is later sold, perhaps much later.

The tax law changes introduced by the Jobs and Growth Tax Relief Reconciliation Act of 2003 (JGTRRA) appear to add further advantages to restricted stock because of the now somewhat greater differential between ordinary income tax rates (35 percent at a maximum) and the long-term capital gains tax rate (15 percent), which can be invoked by the Section 83(b) election. Another provision of the 2003 law capped the tax rate on dividends at 15 percent. But that 15 percent rate doesn't apply to any "dividends" paid on restricted stock before the restrictions lapse. According to tax law, those amounts are not true dividends, as paid to shareholders, but rather compensation that happens to equal the value of the dividend payout. Until the restrictions lapse on restricted shares, they aren't considered true shares for tax purposes. For the same reason, "prelapse" dividends don't qualify as investment income for purposes of deducting investment interest. Because these payments are compensation income, however, they qualify as the basis for various retirement-plan contributions. If your client can't otherwise get to the maximum contribution, don't overlook this additional opportunity.

Unless your client makes the election, the value of the stock when the restrictions lapse will be considered ordinary compensation income and will be taxed at that time, even if he continues to hold the stock. If, for example, the restrictions lapse in three years, but the stock appreciates by $10 per share during that time, if your client had made the Section 83(b) election, that $10 could be taxed at the capital gains rate of 15 percent *when the stock is sold* instead of at the ordinary income tax rate of 35 percent *at the three-year point* without the election. That potential 20 percentage-point differential, $2 per share in this example, can be very enticing.

All That Glitters

Under the right circumstances, the Section 83(b) election appears attractive, especially now that JGTRRA has enhanced the absolute capital gains advantage. Still, you should be cautious. The improvement is not as substantial as it may appear. Maximum ordinary-income tax rates were reduced from 38.6 percent to 35 percent, a 9.3 percent change; maximum capital gains taxes were reduced 25 percent, from 20 percent to 15 percent. Your clients now get to keep

85 percent of a capital gain after tax, but they still keep only 65 percent of ordinary income. In relative terms, however, the advantage is largely unchanged. The after-tax advantage of capital gains treatment was 30.3 percent (80 percent / 61.4 percent = 1.303). Now it's 30.8 percent (85 percent / 65 percent = 1.308)—only half a percentage point better.

A continuing impetus to making a Section 83(b) election within its brief thirty-day window is the expectation—at least for employees in an early stage of their career—that their ordinary income tax rates will increase by the time the restrictions lapse. This tax-rate arbitrage (pay tax early at a low rate to avoid paying it later at a higher one) might in itself justify accepting the forfeiture risk. But large rate increases are now rare, especially since the Section 83(b) election brings otherwise avoidable ordinary income into the current year, possibly pushing the marginal income into a higher current bracket and thus raising the tax rate that applies.

A more typical and even stronger incentive for the election is the common enthusiasm some clients have about the growth prospects of their company's stock, particularly when the company is young and believed to be growing fast. Here, the prospect of strong future growth, all to be taxed as capital gain, can be nearly impossible to resist, especially if the current value—and therefore the tax to be borne with a Section 83(b) election—is thought to be small in comparison.

Remember also that the client's employer has a stake in this election opportunity. The employer parts with the asset when the restrictions lapse, if they ever do. But the employer's compensation-expense deduction occurs when the employee incurs the tax and in the amount of the taxable income at that time. Consequently, to get the deduction now and in a known amount, employers are sometimes eager to have employees make the Section 83(b) election.

Employers assume, often in error, that employees will be happy to cooperate. A client of ours was the chief executive officer of a small private company being acquired by a large public company. He was to take on responsibility for running a major segment of the acquirer's overall business. Part of his new compensation package was a substantial grant of restricted shares in the new employer, and the employment contract drafted by the new employer called for him to make a timely Section 83(b) election. This was our client's first experience with restricted stock. As we reviewed the overall transaction to evaluate its merits for him, I challenged that provision and explained the consequences that could arise. "We never talked about that specifically," he explained. "I guess they're just assuming I'm going to want to do it. Why don't you talk to them about it?" I did.

The company responded by saying that the stock was really going places. "Of course, he'll want to make the election," they told me. "It's the smart thing to do. Besides, our getting the tax deduction now is built into the overall cost of this deal."

Our client scoffed at that notion. "That tax deduction can't be a big item for them," he said, "but the tax bill is no small matter for me. I'll get them to drop that provision, or I'll negotiate for some other sweetener if they won't budge on this Section 83(b) business. I can still make the election if we decide it makes sense, but I don't want to be contractually bound to do it—unless they make it worth my while."

Not every client is going to be in a strong enough position to negotiate with the employer on the Section 83(b) topic, but this client's attitude is appropriate for anyone making this choice. Your client should expect to be paid, somehow, for taking that action. Making the Section 83(b) election is not always the "smart thing to do."

Risk of Forfeiture

Even the demise of Enron and WorldCom has not fully awakened investors to the grave risks of concentrated stock positions, particularly in the stock of their employer. Managing that risk is, of course, the central theme of this book. But for now, let's focus on the a priori risk of the restricted-stock grant itself. The risks of achieving performance thresholds or continued employment, for example, are completely separate from and in addition to the stock *price* risk underlying the general risk of concentration. Whatever the stock might be worth at some point in the future—even if, as hoped, the price grows substantially and perhaps even more than other investment alternatives—the grantee of the restricted stock may never enjoy it. The restrictions may actually come into play and keep that from happening.

Restrictions can come in many forms. If they're related to performance—either the client's or the company's—that level of performance must be achieved or the opportunity is lost. More often, the restrictions are related to the term of service, in which case the employee must remain with the company for the length of time required. If your client terminates employment (usually for reasons other than normal retirement, death, or disability) before the period is over, he forfeits the restricted stock. Companies don't usually grant stock with long-term restrictions in the years just before an employee's normal retirement age, and no one plans to have his death or disability come to the rescue of his tax and investment strategies. So, at the very least, a Section 83(b) election is a bet in favor of the client achieving the performance requirements or a bet against the client's career flexibility during the restriction period.

Consequently, you need to help your client see that a risk of forfeiture does exist. It must. If there were no such risk, Section 83(b) would not be an option. A riskless grant of stock would be taxable as current income in any event. So a Section 83(b) election makes sense only if the client is highly confident that that risk will not in fact materialize. If your client is not so sure, let the opportunity pass and avoid the prospect of making the concentration problem even worse.

Opportunity Cost

Even if you pass that first hurdle—that is, your client is confident that the stock will not be forfeited—there's another to consider. It's easy to calculate but often even more difficult to surmount. The Section 83(b) election is not free. The client's tax preparer must file with the IRS within thirty days. (See the appendix to this chapter). In addition to this effort and the cost in professional fees, there is the matter of the tax payment itself. Unless the value of the restricted stock at grant was very close to zero (often the case for pre-IPO stock; more on that below), the tax liability is a real-dollar amount that would have to come from the client's cash, available portfolio assets, or a loan. In any case, that tax payment has a cost: the interest charges on borrowing or the expected investment return (opportunity cost) the client could have achieved on the cash or portfolio assets that would be diverted to the tax payment. The "dividends," if any, paid on restricted stock (taxed at as much as 35 percent, remember, not 15 percent) don't help here, because they would be paid whether or not your client made the Section 83(b) election. You must look only to the potential growth in the stock's price to compensate for the client's cost of the election.

Unlike stock options, restricted shares don't enjoy any structural leverage that gives them an investment advantage over other assets (see chapter 3). Restricted shares compete with other investment opportunities on the same track and from the same starting point but often with a serious handicap: they can't count their dividends because those dividends are paid in any event, whether or not the Section 83(b) election is made. Restricted stock, therefore, suffers a disadvantage in overcoming the opportunity cost of the Section 83(b) election, because the shares must do so solely on price appreciation. Consequently, to justify making the election, your client must be confident that the restricted stock's growth in value by the time the restrictions lapse, if ever, will be at least enough to break even with the opportunity cost of the election, compounded over the full intervening period. And, of course, your client must remain confident that the restrictions will, in fact, lapse. Clients' confidence in being spared that threshold forfeiture risk often wanes once they've calculated the price tag of accepting that risk over the full forfeiture period. And this, of course, is the minimum price increase required. *Any* decline in price—which is the fundamental risk of a concentrated position—would make the Section 83(b) election a dreadful mistake.

Figure 6.1 illustrates the break-even analysis for stock worth $10,000 at grant for an employee in the maximum federal tax bracket, with a five-year restriction period and a 6 percent after-tax opportunity rate. Under these circumstances, the stock must appreciate at a rate of at least 9.75 percent per year.

In Figure 6.1, anything less than a 9.75 percent compound rate of growth in the stock price would fail to compensate the opportu-

FIGURE 6.1 **Break-Even Analysis 1**

	No Election	**Section 83(b) Election**
Initial value	$10,000	$10,000
Initial tax @ 35%	N/A	(3,500)
5 years' earnings on $3,500 (@ 6% per year after taxes)	1,184	N/A
Minimum required growth in value on shares over 5 years: **9.75% per year**	5,923	5,923
Tax @ 35% at lapse of restrictions ($15,923 × .35)	(5,573)	N/A
Tax on long-term capital gain on sale of shares @ 15% ($5,923 × .15)	N/A	(888)
Net after-tax value in 5 years	**$11,534**	**$11,535**

Source: Kochis Fitz

nity cost. Of course, if that rate is achieved, the stock will enjoy that growth regardless of the election. Except in rare cases of very high visibility, the stock market won't know or care whether your client made an election.

The required rate may seem surprisingly high. If the alternative opportunity rate is only 6 percent after tax, why isn't the break-even stock-appreciation rate only 7.06 percent (6 percent / .85)? The deferral of tax, by itself, confers a significant investment advantage on any asset's growth (see chapter 4). Paying tax early, as your client would do under a Section 83(b) election, creates an initial investment disadvantage. As ***Figure 6.2*** illustrates, by merely matching the opportunity rate—say, 7.06 percent pretax—the election would fall short. If the stock grew at only 7.06 percent, the result of the Section 83(b) election in this case would be a net loss in value of $299, or 3 percent of the initial grant value.

FIGURE 6.2 **Break-Even Analysis 2**

	No Election	Section 83(b) Election
Initial value	$10,000	$10,000
Initial tax @ 35%	N/A	(3,500)
5 years' earnings on $3,500 (@ 6% per year after taxes)	1,184	N/A
Growth in value on initial shares in 5 years@ **7.06% per year**	4,423	4,423
Tax @ 35% at lapse of restrictions ($14,423 × .35)	(5,048)	N/A
Tax on long-term capital gain on sale of additional shares @ 15% ($4,423 × .15)	N/A	(663)
Net after-tax value in 5 years	**$10,559**	**$10,260**
Cost of Section 83(b) election ($10,559 – $10,260)		**$299**

Source: Kochis Fitz

And, of course, any rate of growth, no matter how robust, would be inadequate if the potential forfeiture does occur. Try to avoid getting so wrapped up in break-even arithmetic that the client forgets the threshold question.

A Second-Best Strategy

Even if your client—in the face of all of these concerns—remains confident that there is no serious risk of forfeiture and that the stock price will grow at the minimum rate required, the Section 83(b) election is often still not an optimal strategy. That's because all shares of that employer's stock will enjoy the same appreciation in value that your client is so confident the stock will have. If so, even in the face of concentration risk, it's better to buy additional shares on the market with the funds that would have been used to pay the tax under Section 83(b). Those additional shares will add to the client's expected performance from the restricted shares and create greater total value when the restrictions lapse.

Figure 6.3 adds another layer to the earlier, break-even example (Figure 6.1) to show the improved results of using the amount of the tax payment to buy more shares instead.

Note that Figure 6.3 ignores the possibility that the newly acquired shares may pay dividends, which, unlike the "dividends" on restricted

FIGURE 6.3 **Break-Even Analysis 3**

	No Election	**Section 83(b) Election**	**No Election/ Side Purchase**
Initial value	$10,000	$10,000	$10,000
Additional purchase	N/A	N/A	3,500
Initial tax @ 35%	N/A	(3,500)	N/A
5 years' earnings on $3,500 (@ 6% per year after taxes)	1,184	N/A	N/A
Cost of additional purchase	N/A	N/A	(3,500)
Growth in value on initial shares in 5 years @ 9.75% per year	5,923	5,923	5,923
Tax @ 35% at lapse of restrictions	(5,573)	N/A	(5,573)
Growth in value on additional shares @ 9.75% per year	N/A	N/A	2,073
Tax on long-term capital gain on sale of initial or additional shares @ 15%	N/A	(888)	(311)
Best choice	$11,534	$11,535	**$12,112**

Source: Kochis Fitz

shares, would be taxable at 15 percent. If there are such dividends, the advantages of the additional purchase strategy get even better.

Seeing the Light

Faced with such proof of the weakness of the Section 83(b) election, clients often lose their confidence in the required price appreciation, which was the foundation for this analysis at the outset. That change of heart is appropriate if they already recognize the overall risk associated with concentration in their employer's stock. "Why would I buy *more* of this stock?" they ask themselves. "I already own more of it than I should." Indeed. And why, then, would they make the Section 83(b) election? The results would not be as good.

The apparent glamour of a "special" tax-optimization technique may at first trump a client's normal skepticism about investment optimization. Only rarely have we seen clients go forward with contemplated Section 83(b) elections once they've had the benefit of this analysis. And few decide to buy more company stock with the amount they would have paid in tax. Informed common sense usually prevails. But remember, you have only thirty days from the date of grant to present this analysis and help clients reach this counterintuitive conclusion. If some well-meaning but less-insightful source of advice gets your client's ear and you don't intervene quickly, he may convince himself that he's being quite shrewd in making the 83(b) election.

Complications for Insiders

Clients who are insiders and therefore subject to SEC Rule 16(b) need to pay particular attention to the consequences of the election (see chapter 1). Their ability to sell company stock without penalty or forfeiture of profits is severely limited. For example, regardless of actual knowledge or intent, an insider must "disgorge" any profit reckoned by matching a purchase and sale (or sale and purchase) within six months. To alleviate this constraint, stock option *exercises* and the lapse of restrictions on restricted stock are generally not considered *purchases* under SEC rules. *Sales* of company stock can take place within six months of these forms of acquisition without violating this rule. Purchases of company stock on the market, however, do count and therefore effectively preclude any sale of the company stock for at least six months before or after that purchase. Buying additional stock, then, instead of using the Section 83(b) election, is especially complicated for insiders.

Of course, concentration-risk problems are common among Rule 16(b) insiders, and they're generally the last people who should be looking for opportunities to buy more stock. Still, some clients lose sight of the overall plan. A client of ours held a position in his company's stock and options worth well over $10 million and had agreed to a plan to diversify gradually over the next several window periods. But the day after the stock had taken a small decline in price, the client called me to proudly announce that he had taken advantage of the "buying opportunity" and purchased $10,000 worth of the stock. As gently as I could, I reminded him that that purchase wasn't part of the plan and that we now, effectively, had to wait at least six months before we could sell any of the shares he already owned or could acquire through his options. Although technically Rule 16(b) would cause him to disgorge only his profit on this $10,000 worth of shares, the horrible publicity of being in violation of any securities law, however small the infraction, precluded sales at this point. Very sadly, the price decline continued, precipitously, and that little $10,000 confidence gesture eventually cost the client several million dollars.

The Right Fit

The Section 83(b) election is a second-best strategy even if the client is confident that the forfeiture will not occur and that sufficiently large gains will. But there are two exceptions to that rule.

Higher future ordinary income tax rates. The first exception involves the possibility of ordinary income tax rates being higher by the time the restrictions lapse. Note, of course, that the client still has to be confident that the forfeiture won't occur. But if he is and if the applicable tax rate at the lapse of restrictions were sufficiently higher than at the time of grant and the Section 83(b) election, that election could be a wise move.

Figures 6.4 and ***6.5*** illustrate the benefits of the 83(b) election under such circumstances. In Figure 6.4, with the applicable marginal rate increasing from 28 percent to 35 percent, the election is the winning strategy. But note that the side purchase, although not as beneficial as making the election, is still better than not making the election. And assuming this client, who is in a relatively low tax bracket, would not be subject to insider trading restrictions, that side purchase provides greater interim investment flexibility because he can sell those newly acquired shares long before the restrictions lapse on the restricted stock.

FIGURE 6.4 **Benefits of the Section 83(b) Election**

Rate Increase from 28% to 35%	**No Election**	**Section 83(b) Election**	**No Election/ Side Purchase**
Initial value	$10,000	$10,000	$10,000
Additional purchase	N/A	N/A	2,800
Initial tax @ **28%**	N/A	(2,800)	N/A
5 years' earnings on $2,800 (@ 6% per year after taxes)	947	N/A	N/A
Cost of additional purchase	N/A	N/A	(2,800)
Growth in value on initial shares in 5 years @ 9.75% per year	5,923	5,923	5,923
Tax @ **35%** at lapse of restrictions	(5,573)	N/A	(5,573)
Growth in value on additional shares @ 9.75% per year	N/A	N/A	1,658
Tax on long-term capital gain on sale of initial or additional shares @ 15%	N/A	(888)	(249)
Best choice	$11,297	**$12,235**	$11,759

Source: Kochis Fitz

FIGURE 6.5 **Benefits of the Section 83(b) Election**

Rate Increase from 33% to 35%	**No Election**	**Section 83(b) Election**	**No Election/ Side Purchase**
Initial value	$10,000	$10,000	$10,000
Additional purchase	N/A	N/A	3,300
Initial tax @ **33%**	N/A	(3,300)	N/A
5 years' earnings on $3,300 (@ 6% per year after taxes)	1,116	N/A	N/A
Cost of additional purchase	N/A	N/A	(3,300)
Growth in value on initial shares in 5 years @ 9.75% per year	5,923	5,923	5,923
Tax @ **35%** at lapse of restrictions	(5,573)	N/A	(5,573)
Growth in value on additional shares @ 9.75% per year	N/A	N/A	1,955
Tax on long-term capital gain on sale of initial or additional shares @ 15%	N/A	(888)	(293)
Best choice	$11,466	$11,735	**$12,012**

Source: Kochis Fitz

In Figure 6.5, the change in brackets is relatively small, from 33 percent to 35 percent. The Section 83(b) election remains a better choice than no election, but the benefits still fall short of the side purchase and is still, in this case, a second-best choice.

The client's exposure to tax brackets in any one year is of course a function of the amount of income under consideration. Making a Section 83(b) election could add enough income to move the client into a higher tax bracket in the current year. Any expected tax rate differential between current and future rates could disappear precisely as a result of making the election.

No opportunity to acquire additional shares. The second set of circumstances that could make the Section 83(b) election a good idea arise when additional shares of the stock are not available for purchase in advance of the time the client believes the price appreciation will have occurred. Here, the Section 83(b) election can be an especially attractive strategy. But again, the choice requires confidence that forfeiture will not occur and adequate price growth will.

These situations most commonly arise for employees of companies that have not yet gone public. For them, there is no opportunity yet to use the would-be tax expense to buy more of the stock. The only opportunity to invest more in their employer stock may be to volunteer to pay tax now on restricted stock, thereby establishing a basis for capital gains later. Many clients in start-up companies expect very strong price growth—perhaps very soon—as the company's prospects unfold. For many a would-be entrepreneur, this is the stuff of dreams: restricted stock granted at only pennies per share in advance of a rapid advance in price as subsequent funding rounds occur and, later, an initial offering price of perhaps many dollars per share.

Such dreams, some of them realized, were plentiful at the height of the high-tech and Internet bubble of the late 1990s and in early 2000. For many once-hopeful employees, the subsequent disappearance of many companies with seemingly bright futures and the crash in stock values painfully demonstrated the two unavoidable underlying risks. Forfeiture of restricted stock can occur; and the future stock price can disappoint—massively.

Still, the allure of quick riches is not likely to go away. We should be glad of that. When the risks are affordable and when the potential returns are great, the appetite for such gains is part of what makes a capitalist, entrepreneurial system work. The role of the adviser to recipients of restricted stock is to help them assess their ability to afford the risks of concentration in a single stock and to calculate accurately the amount of return needed to justify accepting them. From one client to the next—and from one time to another—the answers may not be the same.

Appendix

TO: Internal Revenue Service
Fresno, CA 9XXXX

FROM: John Q. Executive, SSAN: XXX-XX-XXXX
100 Maple Lane
Anytown, CA 9XXXX

DATE: July 20, 200X

RE: Election Under IRC Section 83(b) for Taxable Year 200X

On June 30, 200X, I was granted 10,000 shares of common stock of my employer, XYZ Corp., which property will not vest or be transferable by me until the lapse of five years of my continued employment with XYZ Corp. following the date of grant.

On the date of grant, June 30, 200X, the mean of the high and low market prices of XYZ stock was $12.50/share. I have paid no amounts for these restricted shares and am therefore electing to have the entire $12.50/share value (× 10,000 shares = $125,000) included in my taxable income for 200X.

As required by regulations, I am submitting a copy of this election to my employer through the officer responsible for administration of executive compensation, and I will attach another copy to my individual tax return for the year 200X.

____________________________ July 20, 200X

John Q. Executive

PART II

Gifts

CHAPTERS 7 THROUGH 11 shift the emphasis of management of stock concentration to the realm of gifts. Transfers of stock to family, friends, or charity provide many excellent opportunities for clients to merge a number of important goals. Gifts permit clients to be generous with their loved ones, express their philanthropy, and diversify their risks all at the same time.

7 Gifts to Family

Using concentrated stock as a gift, especially to family members, can be a very effective way of joining the goals of investment diversification, estate planning, and the efficient transfer of wealth to loved ones. Clients' powerful inclination to benefit family members often provides the only motivation strong enough to trump their resistance to diversification. Gifts can also bring wholly new decision makers to the concentration issues—new owners who are not hindered by the same legal constraints as your clients. These new owners may also be quite willing, even eager to pay the transaction and tax costs associated with diversifying the concentration risk.

With this chapter, we shift our focus from selling (or not buying) stock to using transfers of the stock as a technique for managing concentration. But before we explore the technique's potential for easing the legal and psychic burdens and reducing income tax exposure, we need to take a sobering look at the estate and gift tax requirements for transferring property.

Transfer Taxes

The federal and many state governments impose both estate or inheritance taxes and gift taxes. The federal estate tax, for example, is charged on the transfer of a client's taxable estate at death, and the federal gift tax is levied on transfer of property through gifts during the client's lifetime. Under current law, the federal gift tax is assessed on a client's cumulative gifts exceeding $1 million.

Separate from any need or desire to manage a concentrated position, a program of lifetime gifts usually makes sense for many wealthy clients in terms of estate and often income tax planning. A program to reduce the size of the taxable estate and transfer property to the client's ultimate beneficiaries can be structured so that each client spouse uses his or her gift tax annual exclusion ($11,000 in 2004, to be adjusted for inflation) and the lifetime exemption amount ($1 million). The opportunity to apply this general wealth-transfer strategy to managing a concentrated stock position creates a compelling argument for making lifetime gifts of concentrated stock.

The federal gift tax law permits each donor an $11,000 (indexed for inflation) annual gift tax exclusion per recipient. That means a client can give as much as $11,000 each year to as many individuals as he or she chooses, with no resulting federal gift tax, and the amount is not included later for purposes of calculating the estate tax.

To qualify for the annual exclusion, the gift must be a *present interest.* Gifts of a *future interest,* such as certain gifts in trust, do not qualify. The law allows married couples to split their gifts, which means they together can make annual gifts of up to $22,000 per recipient without incurring gift tax liability, even if the entire $22,000 is the property of only one of the spouses. A shared marital gift of $22,000 of community property ($11,000 of each spouse's share) requires no gift tax return. When the property is the separate property of one of the spouses and the value of the gift exceeds $11,000, a gift tax return needs to be filed by the couple in order for them to consent to "split" the gift.

A client who was the CEO of a large corporation used the annual exclusion as an opportunity to remove more than $1 million worth of his company's stock from his and his wife's estate and give his family a major head start on building their own wealth by transferring to his four adult children (three of whom were married) and nine grandchildren $352,000 worth ($11,000 × 2 donors × 16 beneficiaries) of low-basis stock each year for three years.

Viewed solely in terms of minimizing all taxes, this client might have sold the stock himself, paid the tax, and then transferred an equivalent $352,000/year value in gift-tax-free cash, thereby effectively increasing the amount of wealth transferred. Some of these beneficiaries were, in fact, in lower tax brackets and therefore paid less capital gains tax than their generous father and grandfather would have paid, but at the cost of reduced overall wealth-transfer opportunity. That minor bit of income tax optimization versus transfer tax optimization had no impact on this particular gift strategy. Nothing would have happened here if the process had to start with the client's selling any of the stock.

Amounts of gifts in excess of the annual exclusion accumulate toward the $1 million lifetime exemption before the transfer taxes apply. When they do, however, the current tax toll is significant, beginning at 41 percent of the taxable amount transferred. For example, if in any one year, your client and his or her spouse were to give a single recipient a total amount of $2,500,000, the federal transfer tax liability would be calculated as shown in ***Figure 7.1.***

In general, when property is transferred as a gift, appreciation subsequent to the date of the gift is not included in the donor's estate and escapes any transfer tax even if the value at the time of the gift is re-included for purposes of the unified transfer tax system. Therefore, property that's expected to produce a substantial amount of income

FIGURE 7.1 **Calculating the Federal Transfer Tax Liability**

Total gift	$2,500,000
Annual exclusions (2 × $11,000)	(22,000)
Lifetime exemptions (2 × $1 million)	(2,000,000)
Taxable gift	$478,000
Tax @ 41%	**$196,000**

Source: Kochis Fitz

or appreciation between the date of gift and the eventual death of the donor is ideal for reducing transfer tax. Wealthy clients typically use stock or real estate to fund these gifts, and highly concentrated stock, whether it's to be sold or even retained, makes an ideal gift.

Making gifts greater than $11,000 per year (or $22,000 for split gifts) is often important for wealthy clients because of that growth potential. For example, assume a married couple owns a summer home worth $500,000 and wants to transfer this property to their child when they die. If the property is expected to appreciate even at only 4 percent per year, it will be worth about $1.1 million in twenty years. If the transfer occurs after the parents died, that value would be subject to estate taxes (if the current estate tax law's scheduled repeal does not occur or is not made permanent). If the property were transferred today, however, the taxable gift would be only $478,000 ($500,000 minus the $22,000 annual exclusion) and no actual transfer tax would have to be paid because a portion of the client's lifetime gift tax exemption would be used.

Even larger gifts, exceeding the lifetime $1 million exemption ($2 million for married couples), can be a great advantage in large estates. Unlike estate taxes for transfers at death, the gift tax on a lifetime gift is not subject to a transfer tax liability on itself. Assume, for the sake of simplicity, a 50 percent tax rate. It would take $4 million to transfer a net $2 million (net of 50 percent tax on $4 million) to beneficiaries at death, but it would take only $3 million of assets if the gift occurs while the donor is still living—$2 million gift plus $1 million tax (at 50 percent rate). Moreover, any gift tax paid that's attributable to any unrealized appreciation in the gift's value is added to the basis of the transferred assets, thereby reducing the eventual income tax burden for the recipient as well.

The assets remaining in a client's estate at death are subject to an estate tax. An exemption applies here too, but since the two tax regimes are unified, the exemption available at death is reduced by any exemption used before then. Therefore, if your client dies at a point when the estate tax exemption is $2 million, after already using the $1 million lifetime exemption, only a $1 million additional exemption would be available for tax calculations at the client's death.

FIGURE 7.2 **Exemptions and Maximum Estate Tax Rates**

Calendar Year	Estate Tax Exemption (less any of the $1 million lifetime exemption already used)	Highest Estate Tax Rate
2005	$1.5 million	47%
2006	2.0 million	46
2007	2.0 million	45
2008	2.0 million	45
2009	3.5 million	45
2010	Repeal	Repeal
2011	1.0 million	55

Source: Kochis Fitz

The estate tax exemption amount for 2005 is $1.5 million. This amount is scheduled to increase gradually to $3.5 million by the year 2009, and the highest estate and gift tax rate is scheduled to decrease from the current 47 percent to 45 percent in 2007. ***Figure 7.2*** shows both the increasing exemption and the declining top rate. Current law provides for repeal of the estate tax in 2010 and for the law to sunset in 2011, bringing us back to the pre-2001 rates with the highest rate at 55 percent and an exemption amount of $1 million.

Although it seems likely to most tax experts that the estate tax factors displayed in Figure 7.2 will change, Congress has left the timing and direction of the changes uncertain. Therefore, your clients' estate plans should permit flexibility in case the law is repealed, or a high exemption is retained, or some other configuration is introduced that one could only guess at today. Creating inflexible, irrevocable arrangements based on present circumstances could turn out to be very unwise. Nevertheless, there is little *tax* risk in transferring concentrated stock before your client's death as long as the amounts transferred don't incur any net tax liability. Annual exclusions and sizable gift tax exemptions provide a great deal of opportunity for tax-free gifts during your client's lifetime.

Income Tax Leverage

Notwithstanding the opportunities to ease considerably the transfer tax burden on the transfer of large amounts of family wealth, the more immediate tax savings from these gifts are likely to come from the income tax. And for managing concentrated stock positions, this advantage is often the more important motivator.

Children or grandchildren are taxpayers in their own right for any money they earn. They also pay taxes independently on their investment income, although special rules, often called the "kiddy tax," can apply to that form of income. Once they reach age 14, however, their tax status is completely separate. This separation permits their investment income to be taxed at rates that may be significantly lower than their parents' rate, including a 5 percent capital gains tax rate.

But even before age 14, a small tax savings benefit applies:

- The first $750 of income is not subject to tax; and
- The next $750 of ordinary income is taxed at 10 percent

Therefore, only the amount of investment income exceeding $1,500 is taxed at the parents' highest marginal rate even for children under age 14.

Transferred appreciated stock, therefore, can be liquidated and reinvested to generate a greater after-tax return for the children than it would for your client and, of course, the appreciation itself could be subject to less capital gains tax in their hands. Given this income tax advantage, your clients should generally make gifts from among their lowest-basis shares, perhaps reserving the very lowest-basis shares for charitable gifts (see chapter 9). Even if your client insists on retaining the concentrated stock holding, a transfer of low-basis shares from the current position can effectively step up your client's basis in the overall holding. The client could purchase replacement shares at full current basis and minimize capital gains tax on the shares given away to family members for whom more advantageous tax rates apply.

Still, making gifts of concentrated stock provides a substantial additional advantage even beyond the potential for tax savings. If your client can use the proceeds of the sale of those shares legitimately to cover an expense that he would otherwise pay in cash, that freed-up cash can then be used to purchase other investments—a painless form of diversification. But this strategy works only for expenses your client has no legal obligation to pay. Providing food, clothing, and shelter for a minor child, for example, is a legal obligation of the parent. College or graduate school education for children and general financial support for an elderly parent, however, are typically not legal requirements. Even funding the difference in the costs of primary or secondary education at private schools versus public education can be a legitimate use of gift assets. But because of the various interpretations of this rule under state law, you should seek the advice of competent local counsel.

Special Rules on Employer Stock

Caution is required when your client makes a gift of employer stock, because securities-law restrictions may apply (see chapter 1). If your client is an insider, as defined by Section 16(b) of the Securities Exchange Act of 1934, a sale of that stock by a member of the client's family may be traceable to the client in determining whether he made a profit through sales or purchases of company stock during a six-month period. The employer's corporate counsel's office can help in making sure a plan for a gift of stock and subsequent sale will be permissible.

Special income tax rules may also come into play. If the company stock was acquired under an incentive stock option (ISO) and held for less than one year, the gift itself could constitute a disqualifying disposition that would generate income tax liability (without proceeds to pay the tax). (See chapter 3.)

Transfer Structures

For this income-shifting approach to managing concentration risk to be effective, the property transferred must legally belong to the child or other recipient. Clients who are confident of an adult child's financial maturity may be willing to sacrifice control. But in the case of minor children, another important matter must be considered: their ability to deal effectively with property in market transactions. Brokers, for example, don't engage in transactions for minors acting on their own behalf. Joint ownership with children or so-called trustee bank accounts fail to solve the problem satisfactorily because income tax savings are generally reduced in these arrangements, and some or all of the assets held in such vehicles would be included in the estate of the donor-trustee or donor joint-tenant for federal estate tax purposes.

Gifts Under the Uniform Transfers to Minors Act

To provide a means of efficiently making gifts to minors, most states have enacted the Uniform Transfers to Minors Act (UTMA). Gifts made in accordance with this statute are treated as completed transfers for purposes of property tax, income tax, and gift tax laws.

Under UTMA, a client transfers cash or property to a custodian to hold, invest, or spend for the benefit of the minor beneficiary. Although the custodian has control over the property, it belongs to the minor and may not be used for anyone else. The custodian holds the property and uses it for the benefit of the minor beneficiary until he or she reaches an age specified in the state's UTMA (typically either 18 or 21, although in some cases it can be extended to age 25 if the account is established as a result of the donor's death). The unexpended balance must be made available to the beneficiary at the specified age or, if he or she dies before reaching that age, to his or her estate.

Your client may act as the custodian. But if the property is your client's company stock, it's generally much better to appoint someone else. This choice will minimize securities-law restrictions. Moreover, with any stock, having someone else serve as the custodian prevents the inclusion of custodial assets in the client's estate in the event of his death while the arrangement is in force. The client's spouse may be the custodian, provided that the assets transferred are not employer stock and are the *separate* property of the client donor. In a community-property state, where the gift is from the community property, neither spouse should be the custodian.

Minor's Trust

Another approach to transferring assets is made possible by provisions of Internal Revenue Code Section 2503(c). According to the federal gift tax law, certain gifts in trust to a minor qualify for the $11,000 (or $22,000 split gift) annual gift tax exclusion even though the beneficiary's right to enjoy the gift is postponed until age 21. For the gift to qualify for the annual exclusion, the principal and income from the trust must be available—at the trustee's sole discretion—for the child's benefit during its term and for the purposes specified in the trust document. In addition, the beneficiary must have the right to a full distribution of all income at age 21. If the child does not make a timely election for full distribution after his or her 21st birthday, the trust may be continued for an additional period specified in the trust. This can be an especially attractive alternative to an UTMA arrangement in a state that gives the beneficiary a right to demand distribution from the UTMA at age 18.

If more than one child is to benefit from the trust, a separate share must be set aside for each child. An $11,000 ($22,000 split gift) annual exclusion will then be available for each child. Your client may serve as trustee of a minor's trust, but this, like the UTMA custodian choice, is generally inadvisable.

Intentionally Defective Grantor Trusts

One of the most important opportunities for tax-effective wealth transfer is the disparity between transfer tax rules and income tax rules. A transfer of property can be final and irrevocable in terms of ownership (thus removing an asset—and all its growth potential as well—from your client's estate) while the income tax liabilities of the property remain with the original owner. We'll see this advantageous disparity again when we discuss transferring nonqualified stock options. Here, the opportunity can be generalized to provide tax advantages for the transfer of any asset through an irrevocable trust for the benefit of your client's intended beneficiaries. Because of the tax advantage, this approach can be especially attractive for dealing with concentrated stock positions.

Income tax rules under IRC Sections 671–677 spell out the provisions, "defects," that would cause a trust—even one that's irrevocable—to have all its income tax liabilities flow back to the trust's grantor. For example, under Section 675(2), if the donor has the power to borrow trust assets without adequate interest or security, even though the trust is effective in transferring the value of the assets from the grantor's estate, it is "defective" for income tax purposes, making it a grantor trust. In such cases, the tax liability for dividends, interest, rents, et cetera, *and* capital gains, revert back to the grantor even though the economic value of all those elements remains in the trust.

When these income tax rules were initially imposed—a time when income tax rates were generally much higher than transfer tax rates—their objective was to limit taxpayers' ability to use trusts to avoid income tax liability. A *defective* trust, therefore, would fail in its attempt to transfer income tax liability to taxpayers in a lower bracket. Now, it's a common practice to deliberately run afoul of the income tax rules and intentionally create a trust that's defective for income tax purposes, so that the income tax—especially any very large capital gains tax liability—remains with the donor.

Here's how it works: A client held a position in one stock worth approximately $2 million, with well over $1 million of gain (see ***Figure 7.3***). Eager to benefit their children and to manage this concentration problem, the client and her husband met both goals by creating an intentionally defective grantor trust (IDGT) for the children's benefit and transferred the stock into the trust. Using large parts of their lifetime exemption amounts, no net gift tax was due on the transfer, and once the stock was sold in the trust, the client was required, as planned, to pay the federal and state capital gains tax of more than $300,000. That income tax payment was not considered an additional gift to the beneficiaries.

FIGURE 7.3 **Advantages of the IDGT**

	Children's Benefit	Parents' Costs
IDGT		
Value of concentrated stock (after tax)	$2,000,000	$1,700,000
Capital gains tax	N/A	300,000
	$2,000,000	$2,000,000
No IDGT		
Value of proceeds of sale (after tax)	$1,700,000	$1,700,000
Capital gains tax	N/A	300,000
Gift of additional assets	300,000	300,000
	$2,000,000	$2,300,000

Source: Kochis Fitz

The advantage of this technique can be dramatic. If these clients had merely sold the concentrated stock directly, they would have paid the same $300,000 in capital gains tax. But producing a net $2 million dollars of value for their children would have involved a total cost of $2.3 million for the parents.

Confirming what advisers have long believed, the IRS has recently ruled that the income tax payment would not be treated as a further gift. In Revenue Ruling 2004-64, the IRS ruled that the income tax payment by the grantor was not a gift to the beneficiaries as long as the trust didn't require reimbursement to the grantor. No well-designed intentionally defective grantor trust would include such a provision.

Family Limited Partnerships

Yet another vehicle used for family wealth transfer and sometimes for the management of a family business is the family limited partnership (FLP). A huge body of commentary is available on this popular technique, far beyond the scope of the discussion appropriate here. Most of that commentary focuses on three key benefits of these partnerships:

- Managing property among family members
- Transferring ownership interests over the donor's lifetime and after the donor's death
- Gaining substantial opportunity to leverage gift tax (and correspondingly save estate tax) by discounting the value of the gift

That gift tax leverage makes FLPs especially attractive for managing concentrated stock positions. In an FLP, your client can move a concentrated asset to children at less gift tax than would apply to an outright gift, because the children would not have a controlling interest in the property inside the partnership and their property (the limited partnership interest, not the underlying partnership's assets of stock) would not be readily marketable. The combined minority discount and lack-of-marketability discount for such a gift can be substantial—a discount of 25 percent to as much as 40 percent is common for something as intrinsically liquid as a stock portfolio.

Of course, what objective observers find liquid some clients may consider very illiquid, especially clients dealing with all the psychological, legal, corporate, political, and tax issues related to concentrated stock. But the dual benefit of achieving a substantial discount on the value of the transferred concentrated stock and retaining some control over how the asset is subsequently managed can go a long way toward overcoming these constraints.

The opportunity for discounting value can be even greater when the concentrated position is itself structurally illiquid. One of our clients was the majority owner of a closely held private business whose other owners were not members of the family but longstanding business partners. Under the terms of the company's shareholders' agreements, the company's formula value was approximately $1,000 per share. But with no market for the company's stock and no right to "put" shares to the other owners (other than at death, disability, or formal retirement), the true economic value of the shares under these conditions could be a lot less than $1,000. Suspecting that there might be a sale of the entire company to a third party within the next several years, this client created a family limited partnership and contributed some of his shares in this private company to it. Discounting for all three conditions—the company's illiquidity, the children's minority interests in the partnership, and the illiquidity of their partnership interests—the stock was valued for the gift to the partnership at less than $500 per share. As hoped for, a third party did materialize some eighteen months later and bought the company for about $2,200 per share.

Your client's delight at being able to transfer assets at a discounted value is matched by the IRS's frustration at the loss of transfer tax revenue. However, the IRS has generally been losing its battle against the family limited partnership. Courts have sided with taxpayers in cases where the partnerships have some legitimate business or other non-tax-saving purpose and have been established and operated in compliance with state partnership law.

Gaining Psychic Distance

Notwithstanding all the tax rewards for making gifts of concentrated stock, perhaps the most powerful value of many of these gifts is the psychological distance they can provide. Clients can easily become less than rational about a particular stock position. They may be overly optimistic about the stock's future prospects or blind to its risks. "This stock has been good to me; it's made me rich," they'll insist. Or, "Its future is still bright. Even if the value went down a lot, I'd still be a big winner. But it's not going to go down."

Right.

A client's family, particularly adult children with some investment savvy of their own and usually with plenty of uses for additional resources, are much less likely to share these rosy views. They would be happy to sell, given the chance. Most clients sense the need for greater objectivity and recognize the wisdom of selling, although they may never admit it. These gift strategies therefore present a tremendous opportunity to capitalize on your clients' natural desire to benefit their family and get them to reduce their concentration risk, to boot. Get your clients to "do the right thing" for diversification by coaching them through the most opportune ways of doing the right thing for their family. Don't force them to acknowledge their own constrained perspective. Cultivate their generosity instead.

8 Nonqualified Stock Options: Gifts to Family

A transfer of stock options to family members presents an especially powerful opportunity both to transfer significant wealth and to reduce the risk of stock concentration. Not only does the transfer afford the client both investment and tax leverage; it also offers an opportunity to substantially discount the gift tax value of intrafamily transfers. But even when significant initial discounting is not available, removing the value of the option spread—which could grow much larger by the time of exercise—from your client's estate can be a highly effective estate-planning technique. What's more, because the person transferring the option remains liable for the income tax incurred on the exercise—and because payment of this tax is not considered a further, taxable gift—substantial additional wealth can be transferred without application of onerous gift or estate taxes. So if your clients are eager to hedge their bets on concentrated stock—reducing risks but preserving some of the upside potential—and if they want that upside to benefit their families directly, transferring stock options can be ideal.

Some stock-option plans permit option holders to transfer nonqualified options to other parties, usually to members of their immediate families or to trusts or family partnerships for the benefit of those family members. This restriction allows this form of compensation to better serve the wealth-building interests of the employee and the performance-incentive interests of the employer. Sometimes the options may also be transferred to charity (see chapter 11). The tax law does not allow incentive stock options (ISOs) to be transferred. If your client, in fact, transfers an ISO, it loses its otherwise favorable tax characteristics and becomes a nonqualified option.

As a technique for managing concentration risk, transferring a stock option has several advantages for clients when the transfer is coordinated with plans for disposing of long shares. Generally, the most appropriate sequence for managing concentrated stock positions of both long shares and options is to sell long shares first and then exercise options to sell their resulting shares (see chapter 3). That preferred sequence applies here as well. Family members should sell their gifts of long shares before exercising and selling options, especially since the gift recipients are not burdened by the corporate political constraints that might encourage holding long shares. Nevertheless, transferring the options themselves long before any planned exercise —or even before any planned sale of the long shares—can be a smart choice.

These transfers become an exceptionally valuable estate-planning opportunity if the value of the option for gift tax purposes at the time of transfer is less than what may eventually be realized by the transferee when the option is exercised and the stock is sold. Given the long duration of stock options (typically ten years), the long-term growth potential in stock value (at a fixed exercise price, with usually no pre-exercise investment cost) can be very large.

This method of transferring wealth is much like any other that hinges on the expectation that the property transferred will grow in value. The routine tactic of transferring appreciating assets before the estate owner's death to beneficiaries, thereby preventing transfer taxes from being applied to the growth in value after the transfer, works for stock options as well. These tax savings justify a wide variety of gift strategies employing the annual gift tax exclusion, lifetime exemption amount, and even the payment of current gift tax (see chapter 7). Nevertheless, there are factors unique to stock options that can significantly magnify these opportunities.

Investment Leverage

Because stock options are typically exercisable at a fixed price, the underlying stock can *underperform* other investment alternatives and still produce superior value for the option holder (see chapter 3). Perhaps the simplest way to see this is to consider the impact of the very first growth (bargain element) in the stock's value above the exercise price. Because no actual investment may be required to capture that value, the "investment return" provided by the bargain element can be considered infinite. But that infinity doesn't last long. Once a bargain exists, the option holder has an opportunity-cost investment in the stock: the profit that could be captured at that point. That investment, however, applies only to the stock's value above the exercise price, where the stock's *whole* value can appreciate. Consequently, the potential gain on that opportunity-cost investment is highly magnified.

Tax Leverage

In most other gift strategies, the recipient is expected to bear the income tax liability on the eventual sale of the gift assets (but see "Intentionally Defective Grantor Trusts" in chapter 7). But the transfer of a stock option does not transfer the income tax liability that will be incurred at exercise. The transferor remains liable for the income tax, at ordinary income tax rates, as well as for any FICA or Medicare taxes that may apply to the compensation income when the *transferee* chooses to exercise the option. Not only is the value of the bargain element itself removed from the transferor's estate, but the income tax liability associated with it is as well, with no transfer tax on the payment of that income tax liability.

This advantage derives from the fundamental tax principle that your client cannot transfer income tax liability on an item of compensation. Internal Revenue Code Section 83 controls the tax treatment of property conveyed in exchange for services, such as stock to be acquired by exercising a compensatory stock option, and fixes that tax liability on the person who is to perform the services, not necessarily the holder of the property at the time the tax applies.

Any gift tax on the transferred option's value is measured in some fashion at the time the gift of the option is complete, but the income tax liability is assessed—perhaps much later, on what may be a much larger value—when the transferee exercises the option. Consider the following scenarios: Your client has an option with a $50 bargain element, exercises the option, pays federal income, FICA, and Medicare taxes of, say, $20, immediately sells the stock and enjoys a benefit of $30, net of all taxes and the cost of exercise. She transfers the $30 net benefit to a family member and pays whatever gift tax cost may apply. The family member now has $30 free of any income taxes, and your client has removed $50 from her estate (the $30 gift and the $20 in taxes at exercise) in addition to whatever gift tax applies on the transfer of $30. Now consider an alternative: Your client transfers the option before the exercise and sale of the stock. In that case, the family as a whole has achieved the same net benefit of $30 (the recipient's $50 value less the client's $20 tax cost), and your client has removed the same $50 from the estate, plus the gift tax on the transfer of the option itself. The crucial difference in this case is that the family member recipient has a value for future appreciation of $50 (achieved at a gift tax cost measured on some value) instead of only $30 (achieved at the full gift tax on $30).

Finally, consider yet a third scenario involving the transfer of that option at a point perhaps long before the exercise transaction, when the reckoned gift tax on the option's value is only, say, $5. In that case, the technique ascends to yet a higher plateau of opportunity by removing $50 from your client's estate and conferring $50 of available value on the transferee but at an initial gift tax on a value of only $5.

Timing and Valuation

To maximize the growth opportunity for the transferees and minimize the gift tax on the transfer, a client should transfer options to family members as early as possible. Revenue Ruling 98-21 (issued April 13, 1998) holds that the transfer of a nonqualified stock option is a completed gift at the later of the date of the transfer or the date the option vests (that is, the date the option may be exercised). It is, of course, possible to transfer an option long before it vests, but according to this ruling, the gift would not be considered complete for gift tax purposes until the option vests. If the transfer occurs after the option is vested, of course, the gift would be considered complete at the time of transfer.

Revenue Ruling 98-21 was an attempt by the IRS to put to rest much speculation about when the gift tax value would have to be reckoned. Some advisers feared that the gift-taxable value would not be reckoned until the exercise date and on what would then be the full value of the bargain element, thereby eliminating some of the estate-planning advantages. Other advisers had argued for a very low valuation on options transferred early after grant, perhaps long before vesting. This ruling, however, bars a very early reckoning of the gift-tax value and is intended, it seems, to preclude transferors from taking into account the required postponement of any opportunity to realize any actual gain.

Ruling 98-21 seems at odds with fundamental property-law principles that consider the option's contractual rights to be an asset even if not yet vested. Numerous examples of marital property divisions, for example, suggest that options, even those not yet vested, are real assets capable of being finally distributed among the parties before the vesting date. Many observers consider this ruling an inappropriate intrusion on state property-law principles and conclude that it may be ignored.

Several clients of our firm have taken this approach, transferring options not yet vested, discounting their value for the risk that they may never vest, and acknowledging on their gift tax returns their decision not to observe the supposed requirements of Revenue Ruling 98-21. So far, we've heard no objections from the IRS. The fact that the IRS may have acquiesced, seeming to allow some taxpayers to ignore the ruling's guidance, however, doesn't protect any other taxpayers from a more aggressive response, particularly if there is a large potential tax liability at stake.

On the gift-valuation issue, Revenue Procedure 98-34 (also issued, and not coincidentally, on April 13, 1998) provides a methodology taxpayers may but are not required to use. This revenue procedure establishes a safe harbor in that the IRS will consider an option properly valued if the procedure's requirements are met. Other valuation methodologies, or rationales, remain available but risk challenge by the IRS. Even adherence to the procedure permits some flexibility, because it requires only that the methodology employed be similar to the one established by the Financial Accounting Standards Board for corporations valuing compensatory options granted to employees (FAS No. 123, 1995). This brings the Black-Scholes option-pricing model to center stage.

Essentially, the Black-Scholes method attempts to calculate the present value of profit opportunity from a publicly traded option—weighted by a measure of probability—over the term of the option. The logic of applying that methodology to employee stock options is dubious at best (see chapter 3). Without a public market for the employee options, there is no opportunity to test the real-world validity of the values Black-Scholes yields.

In any event, for gift tax purposes, the Black-Scholes model is unlikely to be helpful to your clients. It can, to the surprise of many, produce values that are greater (perhaps substantially so) than the amount of any current bargain element. That's because it takes into account the degree of prospective volatility in the stock price. Even though there may be no realizable value today, there could be some value over the remaining life of the option, given the potential swings in the stock price. Black-Scholes provides a probability—and time-weighted calculation of that possibility.

Key factors in the model are the stock's dividends, an investor's opportunity rate, the degree of volatility in the stock price, and any current difference between the option exercise price and the stock's market value. Consider an option at a $10 exercise price for a stock selling at $20 (see ***Figure 8.1***). Assume that the company has announced in its financial statements an expected volatility of 30 percent. On these and other assumptions, Black-Scholes would yield a current value of $11.08 per share for such an option with two years remaining, increasing to $13.88 per share if eight years remained. If the remaining term is held constant at, say, eight years, but volatility

FIGURE 8.1 **Sample Black-Scholes Calculations: Varying Volatility**

Exercise price	$10
Current market value	$20
Remaining duration	8 years

Volatility Expectations	Black-Scholes Values
20%	$13.54/share
30	13.88/share
40	14.47/share

Source: Kochis Fitz

FIGURE 8.2 **Sample Black-Scholes Calculations: Varying Strike Price**

Current market value	$20
Remaining duration	8 years
Expected volatility	30%

Strike Prices	Current Bargain Element	Black-Scholes Values
$10	$10	$13.88/share
25	(5 underwater)	7.98/share
35	(15 underwater)	5.71/share

Source: Kochis Fitz

varies, the value per share would increase from $13.54 for 20 percent volatility to $14.47 for 40 percent volatility.

Varying the bargain element has, as one would expect, a major impact on the value (see ***Figure 8.2***). The eight-year option at a

$10 strike price, with 30 percent volatility, has a $13.88 per share value. If that option were "underwater" (for example, a $25 strike price for stock selling at $20), the option value would still be $7.98 per share. Even if the strike price were $35 ($15 underwater now), the option to purchase—sometime within the following eight years—would still be worth $5.71 per share under the workings of Black-Scholes.

Most clients making gifts of options to family members would do better to decline to use this safe-harbor valuation methodology. Help your clients to consider instead credible valuation appraisals that take into account a variety of real-world discount rationales, such as the risk that a nonvested option will never vest or the option's loss of marketability once it's in the hands of the initial transferee. Additional discounts may be available if the gift of options is itself housed in a family limited partnership that further restricts the recipient's ability to transact with the option or to access its proceeds (see chapter 7).

Depending on the particular client's circumstances, Kochis Fitz has adopted several alternatives to the Black-Scholes valuation methodology. In one case, we used the value of the total current bargain element on the in-the-money options being transferred outright to the clients' adult children. The Black-Scholes valuation in this case would have been much higher—indeed, just under this client's then-available lifetime exemption amount. We figured that if the IRS objected to our valuation technique and insisted on Black-Scholes instead, it would still have no actual incremental gift tax to collect. We never heard from them.

More typically, we arrive at an eventual valuation conclusion by starting with Black-Scholes and then applying several layers of discounts as described above—nonvesting, lack of marketability, and structural (family limited partnership) constraints. In addition to these standard discount rationales is the risk of the concentrated position itself. For vested options, simply exercising the option and selling the shares can eliminate the theoretical risk of concentration. For options that are not yet vested and cannot be transacted in the marketplace, that concentration risk remains. As we will see when we discuss opportunistic concentration in chapter 16, that risk may be just what your client desires. But when it comes time to calculate gift tax values, that irreducible concentration risk adds ammunition for a lower valuation.

9 Gifts to Charity

Just as an adviser can overcome obstacles to diversification by harnessing a client's desire to benefit family and friends, charitable gifts can often come to the rescue of concentrated stock positions. Many people are eager to support the larger community and share their good fortune with those in need. In our experience, one of the most laudable traits of financially successful people is their strong desire to give back, and often very generously. Whether this largesse is driven by some vague sense of guilt, a hunger for status and esteem, or sheer altruism is a matter for others to explore. Whatever its core motivation, philanthropy is real and is usually a significant feature of a client's overall financial portrait. To use your client's philanthropic desires to help manage concentrated stock positions is to win twice.

Tax Savings

Unlike the tax on gifts to individuals, no transfer (gift) tax applies to gifts to a qualifying charity[1] if the donor is living, and charitable gifts at death are deducted before calculating estate taxes. Moreover, making charitable gifts before death lets the donor take advantage of the potentially significant benefit of some federal and state income tax deductions. This income tax savings benefit has many limitations—the most important of which is that the tax savings per dollar of charitable contribution can never be more than the marginal tax rate that would otherwise apply. With current federal tax rates, that means the savings can never be more than 35 percent—and perhaps quite a bit less if the client's taxable income is relatively modest or if it's primarily from dividends or capital gains. In such a case, the tax savings might be at only a 15 percent federal rate.

A further limitation is the cap on the charitable deduction that may be taken in any one year. Under Section 170 of the Internal Revenue Code, the maximum annual charitable deduction is limited to 50 percent of a client's adjusted gross income (AGI), although any excess may be carried over for the following five years. But this 50-percent-of-AGI limit applies only to gifts of cash. If the gift takes the form of appreciated property, like concentrated stock, the annual limitation declines to 30 percent of AGI. If the gift is made to a private foundation, the annual AGI limitation declines further to 20 percent (see ***Figure 9.1***).

Note that the 50-percent-of-AGI limit could still apply to contributions of long-term capital gain property if your client chooses to reduce the amount claimed as a deduction by the amount of apprecia-

FIGURE 9.1 **Limitations on Charitable Deductions**

Character of Charitable Gift	Maximum Annual Deduction (% of AGI)	Carryover (Years)
Public charity		
• Cash	50%	5
• Appreciated assets	30	5
Private foundation		
• Cash	30	5
• Appreciated assets	20	5

Source: Kochis Fitz

tion—that is, to claim only the asset's cost. This may be appropriate if the amount of appreciation is small. Much more often, however, these limitations do come into play, especially when the charitable gift is stock from a concentrated position.

One of the most unusual client objectives we've encountered involved a senior executive of a large public company who retired at age 60 to join a religious order. To enter the order, he had taken a vow of poverty. So, unlike virtually all other clients, who want us to get them rich and keep them rich, this client (let's call him Brother James) needed us to get him poor. It wasn't easy. His business career had been quite successful and in addition to a valuable home, he had accumulated a substantial IRA rollover, a portfolio of diversified securities, and a large holding of his company's stock and options. All together, his net worth was well in excess of $5 million. As generous as he was, Brother James was not about to be foolish with this money, wanting to optimize the total wealth he would transfer to family members, friends, and, of course, charity. It was going to take some time. Happily, the religious order was not blind to the technical constraints involved in getting this done and agreed to permit our client considerable time to achieve an impoverished state.

Our task became one of orchestrating a triangular optimization of IRA distributions and option exercises (to create adjusted gross income), gifts to individuals (he was single, so only a single person's gift-tax-free allowances applied), and gifts of appreciated assets to charity (only 30 percent of that AGI in any one year). As time went on, the values of assets changed, of course, and happily for all, real estate and equity securities prices did very well, including, as it turned out, the concentrated stock. The poverty point kept moving further beyond each year's target expectation, and Brother James paid a good deal of income tax on the 70 percent of his AGI that, over those many years, he was not able to shelter from tax. Because of the reverse wealth-management psychology of this highly unusual case, we had to turn the general sequencing rule of chapter 3 on its head. Instead of selling long shares of the concentrated stock first and then exercising options, we had to exercise options first to optimize giving away the long shares.

The Cost of Charitable Gifts

The case of Brother James illustrates clearly that even making charitable gifts has costs, and those costs can be minimized. Some clients mistakenly believe that gifts to charity are somehow free or that they can even produce net financial benefits to the donor through tax savings. Regrettably, many charities play to this misunderstanding, encouraging donations based on likely tax savings. Those tax savings are real and can be substantial, but they are *never* more than the value your client forgoes by making the gift. Savvy clients and, of course, their financial advisers know that *all* charitable gifts bear a substantial net cost. Charities eager to appeal to a sophisticated philanthropy base would be wise to sing a more carefully nuanced tune.

In the worst case, with no discounting, a charitable gift of cash, with only federal taxes considered, costs *at least* 65 percent of its nominal value (the value forgone less the 35 percent maximum marginal rate tax savings). The cost increases, of course, if your client's tax bracket is lower or if the gift is large enough that its full tax deduction must be delayed (carried over) to subsequent years. This tax savings can be greater if the gift is of appreciated property that would have generated long-term capital gains tax if the client had sold it instead. But even here, the cost is substantial. In the best case, when the gift asset has a zero tax basis, the cost is at least 50 percent of the nominal value, again with only federal taxes taken into account (see ***Figure 9.2***).

FIGURE 9.2 **Cost of Charitable Gift**

Nominal value	$100
Capital gains tax if sold (at 0 basis)	**(15)**
Forgone after-tax value	$85
Tax savings on deduction ($100 × .35)	**(35)**
Net cost of charitable gift	$50

Source: Kochis Fitz

Factoring in the effects of state income tax (larger potential total capital gains tax and bigger savings from larger income tax deductions) can reduce this cost, but even in extreme examples, the total net cost wouldn't be less than 35 percent to 40 percent. And if there is any basis in the holding, the cost goes up (since the capital gains tax avoided would go down).

One ironic consequence—probably unintended but certainly *not* unnoticed—of the tax law of 2002 was to significantly raise this cost of charitable gifts. Formerly, in the best case, charitable gifts cost their donors only 32 percent. Now, as we saw in Figure 9.2, the cost is at least 50 percent of the asset's value (see ***Figure 9.3***).

It has always been the case that donors cannot achieve a net *financial* advantage from a charitable gift. Any assets given to charity are not available to the donor or his family or friends. True philanthropic intent has always been essential to the decision to make charitable gifts. Now, with lower tax rates, generosity must be an even larger ingredient than it was before. Consequently, when your client needs

FIGURE 9.3 **The Increased Cost of Charitable Gifts**

	Before 2002 Tax Law	**With 2002 Tax Law**
Nominal value	$100	$100
Capital gains tax		
(@ 28%)	(28)	
(@ 15%)		**(15)**
Forgone (after-tax) value	72	85
Tax savings on deduction		
(@ 39.6% marginal rate)	**(40)**	
(@35% marginal rate)		**(35)**
Net cost	$32	$50

Source: Kochis Fitz

further motivation to make a charitable gift, the lower net cost of a highly appreciated concentrated stock position and the diversification benefits it promises as a gift candidate may be essential to the decision. So as you pursue strategies to manage concentration risk for your clients, remember that using highly appreciated concentrated stock as a charitable gift is a powerful tool. Even if your client insists on keeping the concentrated stock, he can still give the stock to charity and then acquire new shares on the open market with the cash he would otherwise have given to charity, effectively accomplishing a step-up in basis without incurring tax.

Special Income Tax Considerations

Loss Positions

If your client has a capital loss position in the concentrated holding, it's not taxes that stand in the way of diversification of that position. Charitable gifts won't solve a tax problem that isn't there. Still, some clients would give away loss positions along with the gain positions. There is, of course, a better way. If securities law and corporate politics permit the client to sell shares, he should first sell loss shares to capture tax losses to use against gains elsewhere. The client could, of course, give the proceeds of such sales to charity, but it's generally better for him to keep those proceeds to diversify the portfolio and sate his philanthropic appetite by using only gain shares as the charitable gifts.

Short-Term Gains

Section 170(e) of the tax code does not permit a charitable deduction for any gain amount that would not be long-term capital gain if the property were sold. Generally, this means that appreciated positions must have been held for more than one year to entitle your client to deduct the full value of the property contributed to charity. If the holding period has been less than one year, the charitable deduction is limited to the basis in the stock.

Be careful not to become a slave to this rule. Remember that the purpose of diversification is to protect against *downside* risk. Some concentrated stock positions are sufficiently volatile to warrant not waiting until the one-year holding period has been reached. If the amount of gain is relatively small and volatility is high, it's usually better to transfer more actual value to the charity and have your client get at least a charitable deduction for the basis amount than to risk having both the value to charity and the size of the deduction substantially decline as you wait for the twelve-month holding period to elapse.

Seasoned Incentive Stock Option Stock

The sale or gift (even to charity) of stock acquired by exercising an incentive stock option (ISO) before a twelve-month holding period from exercise (and two years from grant) will disqualify that ISO (see chapter 3). Not only would that disqualification generate direct tax liability to your client for the ISO itself, but also the value of the charitable deduction would be reduced to your client's basis in the stock. That's because if the stock had been sold at the time of the gift, capital gains rates would not have applied to the gain since it would not have been held for the requisite holding period.

Still, capital gains treatment can apply to appreciation *subsequent* to exercise if the sale or gift occurs more than twelve months after that exercise, even if that transaction occurs less than two years after grant (see chapter 3). Such a transaction disqualifies the amount of spread, or bargain element, at the time of exercise but the *subsequent* appreciation could still be okay. Here again, avoid being a slave to the ordinary rules. If the initial gain at exercise is relatively small and the subsequent, year-old gain is large, then a sale or a charitable gift of the ISO-acquired shares can be a wise choice even if it will disqualify that small initial gain. The threat of market price decline can be far greater than the threat of somewhat higher taxes.

Low-Basis Shares

It is very seldom wise to hold even zero-basis shares for a prospective step-up in basis at death (see chapter 2). The opportunities for redeployment, even for an elderly client, are just too attractive. Consequently, your client's lowest-basis shares are the prime candidates for any charitable gifts she makes. In terms of avoided tax, these shares provide the greatest benefit; in terms of minimizing costs, these shares have the lowest net cost of making a charitable gift.

Even with the best of record keeping, clients often present large concentrated holdings that include some shares for which there is no reliable basis information. Rather than guess—or spend any significant time and effort discovering the basis for these mystery shares—include them among the shares to be donated to charity.

IRA Assets

Proposed legislation is currently meandering its way through Congress, which would, if passed, have made financial planning for Brother James easier in one sense and more difficult in another. At present, one cannot transfer an IRA's assets to charity without having that value first pass through the IRA owner's tax return. With the proposed change, an IRA could be directed to a charity and completely bypass any tax liability—or tax deduction—for the owner. Although this sounds like a no-loss arrangement, it could have drawbacks for managing concentrated stock positions.

If taxes were the only obstacle to diversification, your client wouldn't have any concentrated stock positions in an IRA to begin with because no diversifying sales transactions within an IRA are subject to tax. Consequently, no charitable gift of an IRA should ever be needed to solve a concentration problem. But the adjusted gross income created by noncharitable IRA distributions (or by *any* IRA distributions under present law) may be necessary to provide the charitable deduction allowances (50 percent, 30 percent, and 20 percent of AGI) for charitable gifts of concentrated stock *elsewhere* in your client's total portfolio. Be careful what you wish for—or at least be careful how you use it.

Tangible Personal Property

The matter of large, usually illiquid holdings of tangible personal property (antiques, gems, carpets, or art objects) may seem far afield from the issue of managing concentrated stock positions. Still, it's important for some clients to be reminded that for contributions of tangible personal property, if the property is not used by the charity in its exempt activity (for example, works of art by an art museum), no deduction is allowed for the amount of long-term capital gain that would have resulted had the property been sold. That is, the deduction is limited to the asset's basis.

Consequently, clients interested in genuine philanthropy are almost always far better off using concentrated portfolio assets as the gift, perhaps freeing up cash to facilitate the sales or exchanges necessary to cull and refine their tangibles collections. Except for the very finest examples of highly sought-after items, charitable contributions are rarely effective to manage these kinds of holdings

Structures for Charitable Gifts

Direct Gifts

Sometimes, the quickest and easiest way to fund a charitable gift is simply to write a check, especially for small donations. This method also has the advantage of easy tracking and record keeping for tax reporting. But as we've seen, a direct gift of *appreciated* investments is preferable to cash. By giving away long-term appreciated property, your client secures a charitable deduction equal to the fair market value of that investment and avoids paying capital gains tax on the unrealized appreciation. By avoiding the gains tax, your client reduces the after-tax cost of the gift, making gifts of appreciated assets usually much cheaper than equivalent cash gifts.

Transferring the securities is usually a simple matter of transferring the holding from your client's custodial account to the charity's. If the two parties use the same custody firm, this transfer can usually be accomplished in a single day. To facilitate these transactions, we often open accounts for charities with our clients' custodians so the transfer can occur immediately.

In terms of out-of-pocket cost, direct gifts, whether of cash or appreciated property, are less expensive than the alternatives described below, each of which can involve material setup or ongoing administration costs.

Donor-Advised Funds

One of the drawbacks of using charitable gifts to manage a concentrated stock position is that the size of the potential concentrated stock gift is often much larger than the client intends to give to any one charity—at least at any one time. This is a common situation for clients who may hold, for example, a concentrated position of, say, $500,000 in value, who don't intend to give to charity any more than about $100,000 in any one year, distributed among a number of recipients.

A donor-advised fund, an increasingly popular tool for charitable giving, solves this logistics problem and enables donors to conveniently use appreciated securities even for relatively small charitable gifts. Here's how it works: A donor makes a sizable gift of appreciated property (at least $10,000) to a community foundation or other public charity that offers donor-advised funds. The donor claims an immediate tax deduction for the full value of the gift (subject to the AGI limitations). The donor then advises the sponsoring charity on when and how to distribute the proceeds to other charities the donor chooses.

Donor-advised funds also offer flexibility in the timing of gifts. The donor may distribute money to charities from a donor-advised fund soon after the gift is made or over a period of many years. In fact, some donor-advised funds allow the donor to name successors (for example, children or grandchildren) who, upon the death of the original donor, can step into the donor's shoes and continue advising the sponsor charity on the distribution of the family's largesse over even multiple generations. Meanwhile, the charitable gift account can usually be invested in a pool of equities or fixed-income investments that should grow over time, adding to the resources the donor can distribute.

As part of its role as conduit for the donor's charitable gifts, the sponsoring charity takes care of all the administrative work and tracks information for tax purposes. Many sponsors also provide larger donors with assistance in locating and evaluating charitable organizations to receive grants. For the largest donors, donor-advised fund sponsors will often follow up with charities that have received grants to ensure that the charity has used the grant effectively.

Taking the annual AGI limitations into account, a gift to a donor-advised fund in a very-high-income year permits your client to achieve maximum tax advantage, receiving the deduction in the year of the gift. But it still permits the actual transfers to target charities to occur over many future years if that is the client's preference.

Although donor-advised funds are an ideal solution for many clients, they are not right for everyone. After property is contributed to a donor-advised fund, it becomes the property of the sponsoring charity, and the charity is under no legal obligation to accept a donor's direction on charitable gifts. In practice, this is not much of a drawback because the fund sponsors rarely reject a donor's "advice." Doing so would severely curtail future contributions to that sponsor. Nevertheless, the donor has no direct, legal control over the sponsor's decision-making process.

A more significant drawback, perhaps, is that most donor-advised funds limit gifts to registered, domestic charitable organizations. Consequently, most funds are generally not flexible enough for the donor who wants to be directly involved with individual grantees (for example, a scholarship fund for inner city children or support for a specific artist's work) or wants to donate to international charities. Moreover, funds established through community foundations sometimes require that some portion of the contribution be used to support charities in the local community.

Private Foundations and Supporting Organizations

Although donor-advised funds are a fine solution for achieving both concentration-risk-management and charitable-gift goals for most clients; others, with particularly ambitious philanthropic objectives, often require more complex solutions that avoid the limitations of donor-advised funds. Private foundations and supporting organizations are independent legal charitable entities, which can give clients a great deal of flexibility in executing their unique philanthropic vision as well as a more direct role in managing the charitable organization itself.

In a private foundation, the founder, and often other family members or friends, usually make up the foundation's entire board of directors, giving the founder far greater control over grant making, investment policy, and day-to-day operations than is the case with a donor-advised fund.

A supporting organization is also an independent entity, but it's established to support a specific public charity (such as a community foundation). Your client would have a seat on the supporting organization's board, but the affiliated charity controls that board; consequently, your client has more input—a larger voice—than with a donor-advised fund but not the absolute control a private foundation offers.

When helping clients decide whether one of these vehicles is a better solution than the simpler donor-advised fund, focus on the following key factors:

♦ **Grant-making agenda.** A client who anticipates making large or frequent direct grants to individuals (for example, scholarships, artistic grants, assisting the homeless) or non-U.S. charities will generally find that an independent entity offers more grant-making flexibility than a donor-advised fund.

♦ **Permanence.** Some wealthy client families want a permanent charitable-giving vehicle that supports multigenerational grant making and an extended family's long-term philanthropic mission. Although a donor-advised fund can serve this purpose for relatively modest amounts, an independent entity often better serves this purpose when the dollars involved exceed several million.

♦ **Family involvement.** Private foundations and supporting organizations both provide the opportunity for the client's family members to join the entity's board of directors and to participate in carrying out the family's philanthropic vision. Larger private foundations sometimes employ the donor's family members as part-time advisers or even as full-time employees responsible for distributing the family's largesse, making it possible for family members to devote substantial time and effort in achieving their philanthropic objectives.

♦ **Donor involvement.** Certain clients, either because of the size of the gift or the nature of their personality, want to take a hands-on approach to managing the day-to-day operations of a charitable organization. Being on the board of their own supporting organization or private foundation affords donors an opportunity to influence the organization's investment policy, establish grant-making guidelines, retain professional staff, attend periodic board meetings, and perform other functions of managing a public charity.

A supporting organization or a private foundation can also present an opportunity to establish one's social credibility in a new community. Recently, a client retired and moved to a new home several hundred miles away. Three million dollars of this client's very-low-basis employer stock went to fund a supporting organization to the community foundation for the county of the new residence.

A Word of Caution

The sudden, new wealth generated in the late 1990s created a surge in the number of relatively small private foundations. Many of these foundations, however, are now closing down and transferring their assets to less-complicated donor-advised funds and supporting organizations. In part, this trend indicates that the people who set up the private foundations didn't really know what they were getting into. Private foundations must distribute at least 5 percent of their value each year, file annual tax returns, perform audits and complicated financial reporting, adhere to extensive record-keeping requirements, and pay the IRS a small fee for its oversight. In short, managing a private foundation is very much like running a small business. Moreover, because private foundation tax returns are readily available on the Internet, many foundations find themselves besieged with unsolicited grant requests, along with other adverse consequences of their publicity. All of these factors can overwhelm an unprepared donor and require a significant amount of time to manage.

Fortunately, a supporting organization solves many of these problems, because the donor relies on the supported organization's administrative systems to perform most back-office functions as well as to screen grant requests and manage other adverse consequences of publicity. This frees your clients to focus on grant making, while preserving the look and feel of a private foundation by giving clients and their families a significant and permanent voice in the operation and policies of the entity.

Perhaps most important, supporting organizations benefit from the experienced, professional guidance provided by the charities they support. This professional guidance can be particularly important for inexperienced donors who often need assistance optimizing the impact of their philanthropy.

The table in the appendix to this chapter summarizes the key features of these charitable gift structures.

Chapter Note

1. See the IRS publication *Directory of Qualifying Organizations.*

Appendix

Key Characteristics of Charitable Vehicles

DIRECT GIFTS

Grant-making control and beneficiary choice	Medium
Set up and administrative costs	Low
Operational control and investment flexibility	N/A
Privacy	High
Opportunity for deduction now, gift later	No
Cost-effective threshold to establish	Small
Multigenerational	No
Tax deduction limit (% AGI) for cash/LTCG property	50%/30%
Special features and tax-related issues	N/A

DONOR-ADVISED FUND

Grant-making control and beneficiary choice	Medium
Set up and administrative costs	Medium (~1%)
Operational control and investment flexibility	Medium
Privacy	High
Opportunity for deduction now, gift later	Yes
Cost-effective threshold to establish	$10,000
Multigenerational	Yes
Tax deduction limit (% AGI) for cash/LTCG property	50%/30%
Special features and tax-related issues	N/A

SUPPORTING ORGANIZATION TO PUBLIC CHARITY

Grant-making control and beneficiary choice	Medium–high
Set up and administrative costs	Medium–high (~1%+)
Operational control and investment flexibility	Medium–high
Privacy	Medium
Opportunity for deduction now, gift later	Yes
Cost-effective threshold to establish	$1–3 Million
Multigenerational	Yes
Tax deduction limit (% AGI) for cash/LTCG property	50%/30%
Special features and tax-related issues	*Institutional discipline *Philanthropic resources

PRIVATE FOUNDATION

Grant-making control and beneficiary choice	High
Set up and administrative costs	High (~1.5%)
Operational control and investment flexibility	High
Privacy	Low
Opportunity for deduction now, gift later	Yes
Cost-effective threshold to establish	$3–5 Million
Multigenerational	Yes
Tax deduction limit (% AGI) for cash/LTCG property	30%/20%
Special features and tax-related issues	• Excise tax (1%) • Minimum payout (5%) • Family employment • Deduction: —FMV for publicly traded assets —Basis for other property

CHARITABLE TRUSTS (LEAD AND REMAINDER)

Grant-making control and beneficiary choice	Medium
Set up and administrative costs	Medium (~1%)
Operational control and investment flexibility	Medium–High
Privacy	Low
Opportunity for deduction now, gift later	Yes
Cost-effective threshold to establish	$1 million
Multigenerational	Yes, but limited
Tax deduction limit (% AGI) for cash/LTCG property	50%/30%
Special features and tax-related issues	• CLT: Return of asset after lead • CRT: Income stream before passing to charity • CRT: Tax on LTCG gift deferred

10 Charitable Trusts

In addition to the more straightforward techniques for making gifts to charity explored in chapter 9, there are more specialized approaches that use trusts to combine a gift to charity with gifts to other beneficiaries, typically family members. Through a trust arrangement, the donor can also retain an interest in the value transferred. Combining gifts in this way makes these approaches particularly suitable for use in dealing with concentrated stock positions. In fact, many clients and quite a few advisers almost automatically associate one with the other. Charitable trust arrangements come in two basic varieties—the charitable remainder trust and the charitable lead trust. The first is quite well known; the second is not nearly so famous.

A charitable lead trust (CLT) gives the charity an interest in the property first, with the remainder returning to the donor—or to other beneficiaries—after a certain "lead" period has passed. Its advantages are especially attractive to clients who want to eventually recoup the value being temporarily transferred to charity and to clients who want to continue to hold and control a particular stock holding. We'll review the holding advantages of the CLT in more detail in chapter 16, where we'll explore the opportunities presented by deliberate concentration.

In the charitable remainder trust (CRT), the donor or other beneficiaries receive benefits first; the charity gets whatever remains after the interim period, which may run as long as twenty years or for the lifetime(s) of one or more individuals. That means the charity may wait a long time for its benefits.

The Charitable Remainder Trust

On more than a few occasions, prospective clients concerned about concentrated stock positions have announced early in a first meeting that they will certainly need a charitable remainder trust. The first time a client offered this self-diagnosis, I said, "Really? Why is that?"

That first encounter ultimately had a good outcome, but I came to realize that my initial response to the CRT self-prescription was somewhat combative and edged with an impatience that came from my preference for using simple, fast, and low-cost approaches as the first line of attack in solving concentration problems. Still, these CRT requests indicated that prospects recognized, at least at some level, that there was concentration risk that needed to be reduced and that they were prepared to do something fairly elaborate to deal with the problem. So I learned to applaud their sophistication and say instead, "Well, it's really great that you recognize the need to diversify, and a CRT could be an important part of the solution. But let's first explore some alternatives that could be much simpler and quite a bit less expensive."

Acknowledging a prospect's awareness of the problem turned out to be a more effective way to transform those exploratory interviews into client engagements. More important, it helped clients understand early on that our firm was not some financial-product warehouse, with CRTs and other financial whizbangs ready on the shelves, but rather a truly consultative financial-advisory firm that crafted customized solutions by putting each individual client's best interests front and center.

When it comes to CRTs, many advisers fall victim to the same hasty, knee-jerk conclusion as clients do. For many, a charitable remainder trust is an almost universal part of a client's financial plan, especially clients with concentrated stock positions. Indeed, these trusts are so popular that the IRS has even published sample CRT forms (Revenue Procedures 2003-53 through 2003-60) for various fact patterns.

Given the right circumstances, charitable remainder trusts offer many advantages, but they have numerous drawbacks. Chief among them is the chance that a CRT may frustrate your clients' objectives both for their own enjoyment of the property and their goals for charity. Under some circumstances, instead of having it both ways, using a CRT could mean not having it either way.

Tax Requirements and Opportunities

The tax consequences of a CRT can be complex. In part, the arrangement involves a gift to charity (the "remainder" interest), and the value of that contribution qualifies as a charitable deduction for the donor. The donor can either retain the interim interest (either for someone's lifetime or for a period of years) or give it to some other person(s). If the donor gives that interim interest to others, transfer taxes apply to its value (see chapter 7).

For the value of the eventual remainder interest to qualify as a tax deduction, the charitable trust must be irrevocable, as any outright gift to charity would be. Still, the donor can retain considerable flexibility about which charity or charities will be the ultimate beneficiaries. This opportunity for ongoing flexibility about the desired philanthropic direction is an important advantage of the charitable remainder technique.

The size of the charitable deduction as a fraction of the whole value of the trust property is a function of the duration of the interim period, the amount of the scheduled payments during that period, and the discount rate to be applied under IRS regulations under Section 7520 of the Internal Revenue Code. These discount rates change, often monthly, to reflect prevailing interest rates. When rates are low, the discounted present value of the interim payment stream is large; therefore, the charitable remainder portion is correspondingly small. Conversely, when prevailing interest rates are high, the interim payment stream's value is smaller and the charitable remainder's value is larger.

Interim payments from a CRT can take one of two forms: When the payments are a fixed percentage of the trust's initial value, or annuity, the trust is called a charitable remainder annuity trust, or CRAT. When the payments are a fixed percentage of the trust's annually determined value over time, or a unitrust amount, it's called a charitable remainder unitrust, or CRUT.

By being sensitive to prevailing interest rates when establishing a charitable trust and choosing the payment structure carefully, the client can engineer the size and character of the interim payments to achieve an overall investment advantage. For example, if prevailing interest rates (and Section 7520 discount rates) are low relative to what you and your client believe the total return of the trust assets will be, selecting a relatively small annuity amount would likely create a larger eventual benefit to charity. For example, at the 4.2 percent Section 7520 rate that applied in December 2004, a ten-year annuity payment of $50,000 from a $1 million trust would produce a charitable deduction for the present value of the remainder of $596,000. But if the trust's assets actually produced a 10 percent return, the charity would, in fact, eventually receive just under $1.8 million after the ten years of interim annuity payments.

Conversely, in the same, low interest-rate environment, selecting a relatively large unitrust amount would likely produce more cash flow to your client or your client's beneficiaries over time than was assumed by the discount rate, thereby using the initial charitable contribution to leverage the actual interim payment stream.

If interest and discount rates are high relative to your client's return expectations, you could employ the reverse strategies: setting up a large annuity payment to maximize interim cash flows, for example. Maneuvering in this context, however, can go only so far. The present value of the remainder interest must be at least 10 percent of the value of the initial trust assets. For a $1 million gift, for example, if the applicable Section 7520 rate is 10 percent, the annuity amount could be $146,000 for ten years (present value equals $897,000) or $237,000 for five (present value equals $898,000).

Tax Deferral

The charitable remainder trust itself does not pay tax, and that's what makes it so attractive for managing a concentrated stock position. Consequently, when concentrated stock is transferred to a CRT and then sold, no immediate tax is due on the capital gain. Further, the trust pays no tax on the dividends, interest, or capital gain realized on the subsequent investment of the proceeds. To the surprise of some clients, this is not a complete tax shelter but rather a *deferral* of tax. Any amount distributed (whether from an annuity or unitrust payment) carries out to the recipient, first, any current taxable income of the trust and, then, any of the embedded capital gain from the original sale of the concentrated assets.

Here, again, engineering the payment stream can work to maximize the taxes deferred. If the client's primary objective is to postpone as much tax for as long as possible, you might select a relatively small annuity or unitrust amount, expecting most of those taxes to remain trapped in the trust as the funds eventually pass to charity.

Let's consider an attempt to optimize payment structures for a client who established a charitable remainder unitrust as part of an overall diversification program. The client sold his business to a large public company for $15 million, and received payment in the form of stock in the public company. The transaction was structured so that no current tax occurred, but our client's zero basis in the stock of his company transferred to the stock he now owned in the acquiring company. With about $5 million in other investment assets, this 55-year-old was ready to retire from active employment and devote more time to his family, travel, hobbies, and some local charitable work.

The client began by selling $7 million dollars of the publicly traded stock. After tax, that sale produced just over $5 million of investable cash, giving the client a total diversified portfolio of more than $10 million. He gave about $1 million of the zero-basis stock to a donor-advised fund associated with his local community foundation, and he used the remaining $7 million to fund a CRUT, through which the stock was sold and the resulting cash reinvested.

The CRUT was structured to produce a 6 percent unitrust payment for the rest of his and his wife's remaining lifetimes. At the outset, then, the expected pretax annual cash flow was $420,000 ($7 million × 6 percent), more than enough to comfortably provide for this client's core living expense needs. Because the payment was a unitrust percentage, the payment was expected to increase over time, outpacing expected inflation rates, as the net value of the CRUT assets grew. Based on the investment plan we developed for this CRUT, the client confidently expected the portfolio assets to increase, on average, by somewhat more than the 6 percent per year to be distributed. This would accomplish two goals: the value ultimately going to charity would itself increase and very little of the original $7 million of capital gains within the trust would ever be taxed to the client or his spouse.

A very important third goal was to use this CRUT as the relatively low-risk funding mechanism for this client's core expenses, leaving the other $10 million of non-CRT portfolio assets free to pursue more aggressive opportunities.

Coordinating a CRT With the Client's Financial Plan

As illustrated in the example above, in which the client used his CRT to provide a relatively safe, base level of cash flow for himself and his wife, permitting room for risk and opportunity elsewhere in his portfolio, a CRT can be a versatile component of a client's overall financial plan. A CRT can be an especially attractive exit strategy for clients whose concentrated positions offer very little or perhaps no cash flow. Many companies, especially those in industries that are part of the "new economy," pay no dividends. Through a CRT, the donor can extract at least some of the asset's economic value through annuity or unitrust payments without incurring an immediate tax liability but still gain an immediate charitable deduction for the remainder interest. In some cases, it can even be economical to replace the value eventually designated to go to charity by using some of the interim cash flow to purchase life insurance. Consequently, CRTs packaged with insurance programs are very popular with advisers oriented toward insurance sales.

Nevertheless, for many clients interested in both diversifying a highly appreciated asset and making a gift to charity, it's often better simply to give the desired portion of the appreciated investment directly to charity and just sell the remaining position in the investment. The client would have to pay the resulting long-term capital gains tax, of course, but could then reinvest the after-tax sales proceeds in a diversified portfolio. If your client doesn't have a strong, overriding charitable intention for the CRT, its costs and constraints may be far too much trouble. In many cases, the complexity and cost of getting the CRT under way and administering it each year outweigh the benefits it provides, especially for donors whose primary motivation in establishing the trust is merely to defer tax on the sale of concentrated stock.

In recent years, many CRT donors have become frustrated by the less-than-bountiful returns they've experienced with their trusts. During the stock market boom of the very late 1990s, some newly wealthy CRT donors assumed that their excellent market fortunes would continue for the proceeds of the concentrated stock sales. They believed that robust unitrust percentages would permit them to enjoy increasingly generous cash flows as the value of the trust portfolio mounted. Alas, that has not always come to pass.

Some donors have gone so far as to attempt to undo the presumably irrevocable transfer and, so far at least, some courts have been sympathetic to their plight. As long as all the parties agree—that is, the interim beneficiaries, the charity, and the state attorney general (the official guardian of all charitable entities)—the courts have permitted a simple, straightforward division of the respective interests and allowed each of the parties to walk away with intact pieces of the whole. The charity, for example, takes its share and the donor or other interim beneficiary recoups the present value of the payment stream—and incurs the taxes attributable to that much income.

It's comforting to know that there may be a way out of a CRT that isn't working out as planned, but the fix is cumbersome, expensive, and subject to the will of government officials. What's more, the about-face is a reminder that your client could have accomplished the same result at the outset at a cost of far less time and money and without having to wade through a great deal of inconvenient complexity along the way. So if your client wants both to benefit charity and to retain some portion of the concentrated wealth, it may be better simply to parse out the whole at the start. Transfer some of the shares directly to charity (outright or through the deferred-decision vehicles described in chapter 9), sell the remainder, pay the tax, and move on.

The Charitable Lead Trust

Charitable lead trusts also come in two versions. When interim payments from a charitable lead trust take the form of an annuity, the trust is called a charitable lead annuity trust (CLAT); when they're paid as a unitrust, it's called a charitable lead unitrust (CLUT). Like CRTs, charitable lead trusts must adhere to the discounting rates specified in Section 7520 of the Internal Revenue Code. Their tax consequences, however, are markedly different from those of a CRT. Indeed, with a CLT, the tax consequences also vary depending on who the ultimate beneficiary is.

If the donor is the beneficiary to receive benefits following the charity, the donor receives a tax deduction for the present value of the charitable lead interest (which would be relatively large when interest rates are low and relatively small when rates are high) but continues to pay tax on all of the trust's income along the way.

As we'll see again in chapter 16, clients who want to retain a concentrated stock position that generates relatively little income but who seek a large current tax deduction may find a CLT useful. They can use a CLT to reduce overall portfolio risk or to increase current cash by freeing up income tax savings from the charitable deduction (to spend or reinvest) while continuing to hold the stock. Unlike the constraint on charitable remainder trusts, the duration of the charitable lead in a CLT has no maximum time limit. That means that even a minimal annual payment can be engineered to produce a large current deduction if the lead period is long enough. If the Section 7520 rate is 5 percent, even an annuity payment to charity of just $5,000 per year would produce a charitable deduction of nearly $77,000 up front, in the year of the initial gift, for a thirty-year annuity.

When charitable lead trusts are used to manage the *transfer* of concentrated stock, the eventual beneficiaries are not the donor but usually family members instead. Gift taxes apply, as they would for any other gift to family, but in this case, the value of the taxable gift is reduced by the present value of the charity's interim interest. So if your client's plan is to postpone the beneficiaries' actual receipt of benefits to some later time, it may be very worthwhile to insert a charity as beneficiary in the meantime. Not only does this reduce the current gift tax burden on the gift; it also continues to reduce the tax on the trust's income. Unlike the situation in which the donor is also the eventual remainder beneficiary, when the remainder goes to persons other than the donor, the donor has no current charitable tax deduction and no ongoing income tax liability. The assets have been completely given away. Instead, the trust is responsible for the tax liability during the lead period, but with tax deductions to the trust each year for the actual interim distributions to charity (see ***Figure 10.1***).

FIGURE 10.1 **Tax Treatment of Charitable Lead Trust**

	CLT REMAINDER INTEREST	
	Returns to Donor	**Transferred to Someone Else**
Donor receives initial tax deduction	Yes	No
Remainder gift is taxable	N/A	Yes
Value of gift is offset by charitable lead	N/A	Yes
Donor pays tax on interim earnings	Yes	No
Trust pays tax on interim earnings	N/A	Yes
Trust gets tax deduction for charitable distributions	N/A	Yes

Source: Kochis Fitz

Because of these tax features, CLTs are best used for charitable giving in two situations. The first is when the donor has exceptionally large income in one year and wants to collapse several years' worth of charitable deductions into that high-income-tax year, although donor-advised funds, described in chapter 9, can provide the same result in a less-complicated way. The second is to use a CLT to avoid taxable income (for example, the income generated by the property transferred into the trust) by diverting it temporarily to charity when the donor intends eventually to pass property to other beneficiaries. This strategy works particularly well when a client can't otherwise benefit from taking the charitable deductions herself—because she would continually exceed the annual charitable-deduction limitations—and is optimistic that the trust's returns will, in fact, be higher than the discount rates that apply when the trust is established. Any return in excess of the annuity or unitrust payments made to the charity will eventually belong to the post-charity beneficiaries with no additional transfer tax.

A client who was a single parent transferred $2 million to a CLT, naming her two adolescent daughters as the remainder beneficiaries. This trust was funded primarily with very low-basis company stock. She was quite optimistic about how well this stock would continue to do and wanted to maximize the tax-free opportunity to get that wealth into her daughters' hands. For obvious reasons, now was not the time to do that. By setting the annuity trust percentage at 5 percent, for a period of twenty years, the present value of the charitable lead, using the 6 percent return expectation of Section 7520 at the time (May 2002), was just under $1,147,000.

To make sure that the CLT could make its required $100,000 annual charitable payments without having to sell any of the company stock, the trust was funded with $1.25 million of that stock and $750,000 of other appreciated and appreciating assets. Those other assets would be liquidated first to meet the charitable funding needs to whatever extent their dividends and the dividends on the company stock fell short. This $1,147,000 charitable gift value left only $853,000 to be currently taxed as the present value of the remainder interest to be paid to the girls twenty years later. That amount was well below our client's $1 million lifetime exemption amount. Our client, of course, anticipated the stock would perform far better than the 6 percent Section 7520 discount rate at that time, so she expected her daughters to win big, but at a more appropriate time in their lives.

As this example illustrates, charitable lead trusts are mostly *not* about philanthropy but about minimizing the costs of transferring assets to other beneficiaries when some delay is either acceptable or desired. Consequently, CLTs can be very useful for managing the tax-effective transfer of concentrated stock to the benefit of family members, particularly when interest rates are low and the calculated value of the interim charitable interest is high.

11 Nonqualified Stock Options: Gifts to Charity

Using nonqualified stock options as gifts to family members presents an especially effective way to manage the risk of a concentrated stock position (see chapter 8). When the recipient of the gift is a charity, the results can be even more interesting. Of course, the client's stock-option plan must permit such a transfer, or at least those in charge of it must be willing to acquiesce in a client's purported transfer to charity even if the terms of the plan make no direct provision for it.

As with gifts to family, by law only nonqualified options may be transferred to a charity; incentive stock options (ISOs) may not. This exclusion doesn't mean that their transfer is impossible; it merely means that the client forfeits the special income tax treatment available to ISOs if they're transferred. In tax parlance, transferring an ISO "disqualifies" the option's incentive features, and it becomes merely a nonqualified option. As is the case with a family gift, transferring options remains feasible even if your client has been granted only the generally very favorable ISO variety of options. Thanks, but no thanks. For options your client wants to transfer, merely disqualify as many ISOs as necessary to achieve the desired transfer result.

The Charitable Gift

The charitable gift presents an opportunity to put the IRS's "safe-harbor" valuation methodology to a client's substantial advantage. We reviewed in chapter 8 the weaknesses of the Black-Scholes option-pricing methodology as applied to employee stock options and presented several arguments advisers can use to avoid that valuation technique in measuring *gift tax* exposure. With charitable gifts, however, your client's perspective on valuation reverses, as he seeks as high a value as can be reasonably justified. The safe-harbor valuation regime of Revenue Ruling 98-34 can be quite helpful here because it typically produces a high value relative to the current income-taxable spread. As illustrated in chapter 8, an option with an exercise price of $10 for stock selling at $20, with eight years remaining before expiration and a high level of expected volatility (40 percent), would generate a Black-Scholes value of $14.47 where the current bargain element is only $10. In such a case, the option holder could capture only $6.50 per share from the option itself ($10 bargain element less 35 percent federal tax) but could put $10 into a charity's hands at a net cost of only $4.94 (see ***Figure 11.1***).

Of course, as with all gifts to charity, a client would also want to avoid any discounting theory; so only vested options would be given away. And to maximize the valuation, it's best to transfer those

FIGURE 11.1 **Valuation Leverage**

	Keep Option	**Transfer to Charity**
Retained/(forgone) value (pretax)	$10.00	($10.00)
Tax on exercise (@ 35%)	(3.50)	N/A
Tax savings on charitable deduction ($14.47 × .35)	**N/A**	**5.06**
After-tax wealth	$6.50	($4.94)

Source: Kochis Fitz

options with the lowest exercise prices and the longest remaining terms. Again, in making gifts to charity, the outcome your client seeks in valuing the options is turned on its head. Compared with the results desired in making gifts to family members, here the motivation is to maximize the valuation.

Mismatches of Valuation and Timing

In gifts of stock options to charity, the difference between the size of the tax deduction for the donor and the amount actually available to the charitable recipient is potentially very large, ironic as that may be. As illustrated in Figures 8.1 and 8.2, the Black-Scholes valuation formula can produce a value much larger than the current income-taxable option spread. The younger the option (thus the more time remaining in its term), the smaller the current spread, and the more volatile the stock's price history has been, the greater that Black-Scholes value will be. Nevertheless, the amount of the spread at the time of exercise is all the value the charity can actually capture. If your client's objective is solely to maximize the size of the charitable deduction, regardless of what the charity can realize, this likely imbalance may not be a problem. A deduction for $13 or $14 per share when the charity can only capture $10/share, for example, may be just fine with the client.

Even so, your client must face the adjusted gross income (AGI) limitations for charitable contributions, which in this case is 50 percent of that AGI. When the charity exercises the option, the donor will incur ordinary compensation income, thereby increasing the AGI in the year of the exercise, but the additional AGI will equal only the amount of the spread. The Black-Scholes–enhanced charitable gift valuation could be considerably more than 50 percent of that increased AGI, which would require your client to rely on deducting unused charitable contributions during the five years following the initial charitable gift. This potential delay in being able to use the deduction could seriously diminish the value of the initial donation for your client.

Less important in most cases is the possible mismatch in timing. Your client must deduct the charitable contribution amount in the year he makes the contribution. The charity's *exercise* of that donation could be much later, especially if the donor was eager to have the option's leverage come into play by planning a delay in that exercise—and therefore a delay in the addition to the client's AGI caused by the exercise. Most independent charities, however, are not likely to gamble on the future potential of a currently available option spread and risk losing the amount of spread available at the time of the gift. The charity will want to capture the bird in the hand and exercise an in-the-money stock option virtually immediately. In such cases, the taxable income to the donor, the tax deduction for the donor, and the benefit to the charity are likely to occur in the same tax year, even if all three amounts are not the same.

Why Bother?

The possible exaggeration in the value of the deduction for such a gift is tempting, but is it enough to make the transaction worthwhile? Except for that potential valuation difference, you could achieve the same fundamental results merely by having the client exercise the option, sell the shares, and donate the proceeds to charity. Still, that outsized charitable deduction can be compelling. The example in ***Figure 11.2*** assumes a client has options on 10,000 shares at a $10/share exercise price when the stock is selling at $20/share. The client is in the 35 percent maximum federal tax bracket and can fully absorb very large charitable contribution deductions in the current year. Because the options have several years left to run and the stock price is highly volatile, the Black-Scholes valuation for these options is $22/share.

Gifts of stock options can make sense for other reasons as well, having nothing to do with taxes. Analysts, shareholders, media, and regulators scrutinize many corporate executives with heightened vigor, especially in the wake of Enron and WorldCom. Many of these observers lack the insight or the patience to look beyond appearances to see the economic equivalence of these two ways of achieving the same result: reducing stock concentration and providing charitable benefits in one set of transactions. Giving options to charity and then bearing the "penalty" of tax when the charity exercises could seem much less objectionable—even laudable—whereas the quick exercise and sale can appear to be another example of short-term execu-

FIGURE 11.2 **Advantage of Option Transfer**

	BENEFIT TO CHARITY	COST TO CLIENT
A. Client exercises options, sells, and donates proceeds		
Gross value ($20 – 10 × 10,000)	$100,000	($100,000)
Tax on exercise	N/A	(35,000)
Value of tax deduction ($100,000 × .35)	N/A	35,000
Net	$100,000	($100,000)
B. Client transfers options; charity exercises and sells		
Gross value	$100,000	($100,000)
Tax on exercise	N/A	(35,000)
Value of tax deduction ($22 × 10,000 × .35)	N/A	77,000
Net	$100,000	($58,000)
Advantage to transfer		**$42,000**

Source: Kochis Fitz

tive enrichment at the expense of shareholders' long-term interests. What's more, the company-imposed executive shareholding requirements and the securities-law constraints described in chapter 1 could from time to time effectively preclude the executive's exercise and immediate sale of shares. But the transfer of options to an independent charity, like the charitable transfer of the shares themselves, can be almost entirely free of that onus. The transfer itself would require reporting, but the report would reflect the charitable recipient. The subsequent decision about whether and when to exercise, as well as the capture of the wealth, would all be in safe hands.

Charities Close to Home

A charity's independence—or perceived lack of it—has a considerable effect on the timing questions and on shielding the donor from regulatory burdens or bad publicity. Transferring options to a *self-trusteed* charitable remainder trust (CRT) or a private foundation not only fails the independence test but also puts the client at risk of running afoul of special self-dealing rules. Those rules are reason enough for your clients not to serve as the sole trustee of a CRT or private foundation they may establish. But if the CRT or foundation has an independent trustee who will at least consider your client's recommendations, then options can make a very appealing gift for the truly philanthropic client.

Remember the powerful investment leverage that options present. If your client is in fact optimistic about future price appreciation, options, particularly those with long remaining exercise periods, are the best way to reap the benefits of that expected future wealth. If philanthropy is your client's true motivation, he might want that expected wealth to inure to the ultimate benefit of charitable recipients and would thus encourage the independent trustee to defer exercise so that the option's leverage has more time to achieve that greater wealth. That independent trustee, of course, must act in appropriate fiduciary fashion, but given the right circumstances, that could include a long delay in exercise, yielding, the trustee would hope, a much larger spread. If that good result in fact occurs, the original donor will then be liable for much greater tax, with no charitable deduction that corresponds either in timing or amount. The donor took that deduction, whatever it was, in the year the options were originally transferred. That's why this "delay exercise" strategy works only for a client who has true philanthropic intent and is free to take—or to encourage an independent trustee to take—the continued risk of the concentrated position.

For the client contemplating a gift of options to such a "home" charity, the conclusion that continued concentration risk is affordable is probably easy to reach. If your client has already solved the basic concentration problem through sales, outright gifts, or a CRT initially funded with long shares of the concentrated stock, the options, as an additional element, may well be an affordable risk. This is likely to be especially true for a private foundation because a client with a private foundation is probably wealthy enough, in absolute terms, that the continued concentration risk of the options is far less likely to be a problem. Still, the independent trustee(s) must separately conclude that it's not a problem for the trust and its charitable beneficiaries. Perhaps he will.

The Wealth Effect

Stock options are an exceptionally powerful tool for creating wealth for their holders, but their use as a gift has broader ramifications. Many clients have become quite wealthy as a result of option exercises; many more will do so over time. It is this wealth, rather than the options themselves, that creates the opportunity for charitable largesse. Whatever the client's net worth starting out, however, the capture of additional wealth can foster the motivation needed to consider doing *more* for the public good. What's more important, the additional wealth from options frees up other assets to give away. As we saw in chapter 9, appreciated assets, which bring relief from capital gains taxes when given to charity, remain the prime candidate for charitable gifts. For most clients, options don't make the gift; they make the gift more affordable.

PART III

Retention

CHAPTERS 12 THROUGH 16 describe the array of techniques for optimizing a concentrated stock position in which the client either must retain the holding or, for good reasons or bad, chooses to pursue the risk. Here, advisers must leave their own bias at the door. Recognize that *your* objective must be to help your clients accomplish *theirs.* But when concentrated stock is being retained, your expertise and technical skill can often be the most helpful. Even a "stand still" position can usually be improved upon by refinements around the edges.

12 Margin: An Acquired Taste

Of all the approaches to managing concentrated stock positions, strategies that involve retaining the stock are easily the most controversial. And using margin (debt) as part of the retention strategy may be the most controversial choice of all. Many advisers (and their clients), focusing primarily on the increased risk that margin generally entails, consider it something to be avoided under nearly all circumstances. But when it comes to a concentrated stock position, there is no reason to reject margin out of hand.

Many advisers consider the use of margin practically risqué, not something that comprehensive financial advisers concerned about the long-term welfare of their clients would bring up in polite discourse, never mind weave into a financial plan. But a few advisers—and quite a few clients—see margin as especially astute, a way to maximize profit. Well, which is it? It depends, of course, on the return appetites and risk tolerance of the client.

Margin acquired its bad reputation from those who used it to increase the return potential—and accordingly the risk—of a position intended to be concentrated. In the final stages of the Internet bubble in the late 1990s and early 2000, for example, many eager paper millionaires borrowed on margin to buy *more* of their employer's stock or to exercise and *hold* option stock. When stock prices fell, margin calls caused these disillusioned borrowers to add new funds to cover the debt or to sell the margined stock at what they continued to believe were temporarily depressed prices. Many people lost a great deal—not only did the expected stock gains never materialize but the debt had to be repaid as well. Even as dire an option as bankruptcy is no help in these extremes. The margin lender (broker) holds the collateral (stock) for the loan and must, by law, sell it if necessary to avoid a default on the margin loan.

Living on such an edge is not what I have in mind. Many of our clients use some margin to enhance the net long-term returns of a broadly diversified portfolio. And sometimes we do encourage clients to use margin to acquire a single stock or other asset as a deliberate exercise in a high-risk, high-return strategy. But they take such moves only after they've set aside lower-risk assets in amounts more than adequate to achieve their most important objectives. As we'll explore in chapter 16, opportunistic concentration, even when augmented by margin, is a legitimate strategy for the right client in the right circumstances. But that's not the client we're talking about here. This chapter is about what to do for the client who wants to reduce the risk of a concentrated holding but can't or won't sell the stock or give it away. Using the existing concentrated holding as the collateral for margin borrowing, you can help manage the risk of that refusal in several ways.

Margined Diversification

It's especially important for advisers to guard against the temptation to project their own tolerance for risk or their own feelings about financial propriety onto their clients. Strive instead to discover your client's actual tolerance for risk. And know that that tolerance is not static; it's driven by necessary or desired outcomes, and a client can learn to raise the bar. And in the context of managing the retention of a concentrated—and therefore risky—stock position, clients can see the necessity of choosing *where* they're willing to accept risk. If they dislike using margin as the simplest way of managing the risk of retaining a concentrated stock position, they can—and sometimes do—change their minds about accepting the stock's concentration risk at all. An outright sale or a gift may be seen as the better choice, after all.

Logistics

A margin strategy requires some preparation. You've got to first deposit the shares in a brokerage account that's defined as "marginable." Unlike a cash account, the broker can lend assets from a margin account to other investors. In general, this use of the funds is of no concern to your client because the broker will provide all features of your client's ownership of the assets even while they're on loan to others. There is one exception to this, which became important after the tax law changed in 2003. If your client's stock pays a dividend, the "dividend-equivalent" payment your client receives from the borrower of the stock will not qualify for the new 15 percent maximum rate on true dividends. If this new rate survives at all, further refinement to the tax law may cure this probably unintended restriction. In the meantime, however, you must factor this loss of the maximum rate of 15 percent tax on dividends into your analysis of the costs of margin borrowing.

A margin account automatically gives the client access to margin borrowing from the broker, with no further application or approval required. The collateral for the loan is already in the broker's custody, and the terms of the account give the broker the power to execute on that collateral if necessary. That's not to say there's never a need or an opportunity to negotiate with the broker. Margin interest rates reflect the broker's cost of funds and an acceptable level of profit. These amounts are sensitive to the client's volume of borrowing. Unlike other loan arrangements, in which the cost of borrowing often goes up as the size of the loan increases (in line with the lender's perception of the increased risk of not being repaid), margin loans enjoy a volume discount. With margin accounts, the lender (broker) is not concerned about being repaid; it holds the collateral. So as the amount of margin goes up, the cost per dollar can go down.

Whether a stock is marginable at all, and to what extent, sometimes requires negotiation with the broker. Such uncertainty is

FIGURE 12.1 **Maximum Initial Margin Debt**

Collateral position (concentrated stock)	$100,000
Diversified assets purchased on margin	100,000
Gross value of account	$200,000
Margin balance (50%)	(100,000)
Net equity (50%)	$100,000

Source: Kochis Fitz

often the case for stock with little trading history, such as shares from a newly public company. The broker may be ready to accept the stock as collateral only to a very limited extent—or not at all. With stock from a well-established company, the normal margin opportunity permits margin borrowing of as much as 50 percent of the account value at the outset. For example, if the full margin balance was invested in diversified assets to be purchased within the account, the initial margin balance could *equal* the value of the initial concentrated collateral position at the time of borrowing, yielding a margin balance of 50 percent—or net account equity of 50 percent (see ***Figure 12.1***).

For margin calls, the net equity (initially at least 50 percent of the account) can fall below 50 percent, but it can generally be no less than 35 percent, which is the typical "maintenance margin" limit.

Margin and Liquidity

Perhaps the most obvious benefit of using margin collateralized by concentrated stock is that it makes the expanded portfolio position more liquid. The client, who may be reluctant or unable to sell the stock from the concentrated position itself, can now sell diversified assets to produce cash.

To capture cash proceeds, however, your client must first move the assets to be sold into a separate account and leave sufficient total assets in the margin account to meet the maintenance margin requirement. He then executes the sale within that separate account. A sale within the original margin account would merely reduce the margin balance; that is, the broker uses the cash proceeds to first pay down the margin loan.

If liquidity is the goal, why not just take the margin loan out in cash? Why bother buying other assets first only to have to sell them in another account? Your client can extract cash directly. As long as the account holder maintains the margin equity threshold, the broker doesn't monitor the use of the margin debt. But the IRS does. If it's important to be able to deduct the margin interest expense, the purpose for the borrowing matters, because not all loans qualify.

Interest on personal loans is not a deductible expense, but interest on a loan used to purchase investment assets is deductible as long as certain requirements are met. Treasury regulations under Internal Revenue Code Section 163 include detailed "tracing rules" to determine whether loan interest is deductible. From a purely economic standpoint, all money is interchangeable: all dollars are equal. But from a tax standpoint, some dollars are holier than others. And if your client wants to achieve the tax benefits of deducting interest expense, you have to play by the rules and be able to connect borrowed money to a deductible purpose.

If you've organized your client's transactions to pass this tracing hurdle, other rules may still limit how much margin interest can be deducted in any one year. Under the regular tax calculation, you can deduct margin interest up to the amount of any investment income (dividends,[1] interest, and even long- or short-term capital gains) plus $10,000. The alternative minimum tax provision has no allowance for an extra $10,000. In either case, your client can carry over any unused interest expense to any future tax year, subject to the same investment-income limitations in those years. Sooner or later the investment interest expense will likely achieve some tax benefit. And that benefit may be crucial in determining whether margin borrowing makes sense at all. Without deductibility, the interest expense of margin borrowing may simply be too high a price to pay for the anticipated benefits.

Reduced Risk

An ironic and, to many, a surprising benefit of using margin to manage a concentrated stock position is that it can reduce overall portfolio risk. Margin debt, of course, unavoidably increases the overall volatility—up or down—of the leveraged portfolio. But upward volatility is hardly a concern. I've never known a client who wasn't happy to have that. The goal of managing a concentrated stock position is to lessen its potential for downward volatility. Margin can help you do that: The concentrated position may have some idiosyncratic volatility characteristics—for example, gold-mining stocks, which tend to rise or fall exaggeratedly with changes in the price of gold, or utility stocks, whose price behavior is similar to that of bonds. If those characteristics can be offset with assets with low or even negative correlation, the aggregate portfolio's downside potential may be less—despite being leveraged by margin—than the downside potential of the concentrated position on its own.

Diversification—that is, aggregating assets that are not perfectly correlated—is of course at the heart of this strategy. If your client can't or won't pursue diversification directly by selling the concentrated stock position and buying other assets, he can do it indirectly by borrowing the money to buy those other assets. But the value of that borrowing must still stand on its own merits. That brings us to the matter of returns, the most important potential benefit of margin.

Enhanced Return

Any appropriate use of margin relies on the expectation—of course, not always fulfilled—that the return on the leveraged assets will exceed the cost of the margin interest. In light of the respective returns of equities and fixed-income investments over the long term, it should. Every adviser is familiar with the historical data showing that stocks strongly outperform fixed-income investments. Most are also convinced of the logic that, in the aggregate and over the long term, the relationship doesn't just happen to work out this way; it must be this way.

But that logic holds up only when supported by two crucial conditions: "in the aggregate" and "over the long term." The confidence that equities will outperform fixed income is justified only in the case of aggregates, that is, diversified positions. Any single stock, of course, can completely fail. Likewise, that confidence requires a reasonably long time frame (the longer the better, but at least five years is reasonable). In the short term, even diversified equity positions can be outpaced by interest costs. That means margined diversification should be used only as a long-term management technique. In the short term, it can fail badly.

Of course, in the long run, diversified equity positions must continue to return more than lower-risk fixed-income positions do or the entire free market for capital would collapse. I, for one, have too much faith in unchanging human nature to fear that will happen. Equity investments, reflecting ownership of businesses providing goods and services, are proxies for the *users* of capital. Fixed-income investments are proxies for the lenders, that is, the *suppliers* of capital. In the aggregate and over time, the users must be able to repay the suppliers—keeping them happy enough to continue supplying—and still have enough return left to make the risk of being a user worth taking, rather than the safer road of being a supplier. Both users and suppliers, of course, are essential to the process at all times, with imbalances in the respective desires to supply or use capital reflected in the prevailing price.

If you share this capsulized view of capital market theory and share my conviction that a diversified, long-term equity preference over fixed-income returns is predictable, you can be brave about encouraging clients to use margin to enhance the expected returns of a diversified equity position to be held for the long term. You confidently expect the returns from the long-term equity holding to be relatively high and the costs (interest) of the short fixed-income (margin) debt to be relatively low, with the difference being additional profit for your client. For example, given the mean long-term returns of large-capitalization U.S. stocks[2] at 9 percent and the equivalent returns on long-term corporate bonds at 6 percent, you could expect a 3 percentage-point long-term advantage if those rates were the outcomes for your client's use of margin. That would be an extra $3,000 per year for every $100,000 of borrowing and diversified buying your client did. With many concentrated positions measured in the many millions of dollars, the net return of margined diversification can be significant.

The actual differential between returns and costs is likely to be even better than 3 percent. There are two reasons for that. First, margin interest rates, which can vary daily, are very *short-term* rates. That means the 6 percent long-term corporate bond average is probably too high an estimate. Although short-term rates can fluctuate substantially and move rapidly—and, for a while, can be higher than long-term rates—the long-range prevailing interest rate for short-term debt should be lower than for long-term debt because of the greater risk of long-term debt. History and logic concur: short-term rates have been and—over the long term—must necessarily be lower than long-term rates.

The second reason that net returns are likely to exceed 3 percent has to do with taxes. If the margin interest expense is deductible at all, it's deductible at generally higher rates than the rates at which the returns are taxed. At today's maximum federal income tax rates, the interest expense would be deductible at 35 percent (regular tax) or 28 percent (alternative minimum tax). Much—and perhaps all—of the return expected from the diversified equity portfolio could be in the form of long-term capital gains, taxable at rates no higher than 15 percent. The after-tax leverage therefore could be far larger than the pretax.

With these two advantages in mind, ***Figure 12.2*** assumes the equity portfolio yields 9 percent, all in the form of long-term capital gain, and that the long-term margin interest cost is only 4 percent, deductible at a 35 percent rate.

A tax-savvy reader might object that this example is flawed since the margin-interest deductibility, at 35 percent, presumes some offsetting investment income to be taxed at 35 percent and therefore can't include *these* capital gains (or any dividends) if they are to be taxed at 15 percent. And that reader would be right. But even leaving aside the additional $10,000 regular tax allowance, the tax law does not require that the offsetting investment income come directly from

FIGURE 12.2 **After-Tax Margin Leverage**

	Pretax	After-Tax
Return	9.00%	7.65%
Margin cost	4.00	2.60
Leverage (return/cost ratio)	2.25	2.94

Source: Kochis Fitz

the assets purchased with the margin. That income could come from some other investment asset.

Achieving the return advantage of margined diversification mandates that the asset being leveraged be some form of equity (stocks, real estate, private equity, et cetera) that can be expected to outpace margin interest costs. Not only does this mean your client shouldn't buy fixed-income assets with the margin proceeds; it also means he should generally avoid holding other fixed-income assets while the margin is in force. In terms of your client's total portfolio, holding these two positions simultaneously wouldn't make much sense.

Behavioral theorists chide clients and the adviser community for the tendency to compartmentalize portfolios according to different purposes at different times. With great respect for the theoretical correctness of the behaviorists' view, in the real world, advisers deal with flesh-and-blood clients who sometimes insist on choices that are indeed less than optimal. Maintaining large cash or other low-yielding fixed-income reserves while simultaneously using margin is sometimes one of them.

Sometimes those reserves are targeted to the very near term, such as an anticipated tax payment or funds set aside to facilitate a large purchase, such as a new residence. Such cases are not so bad if the fixed-income investment is expected to be liquidated soon and the margin is expected to last a long time.

Other situations are far more complex. Several years ago, one of our clients, a U.S. citizen, took a job as chief executive officer of a company formally headquartered in Bermuda but with executive offices in London. He and his family were to take up residence in London, and the company would pay him about 10 percent of his total compensation in the United Kingdom and the remaining 90 percent in Bermuda—an arrangement that's perfectly legal under U.K. tax law. As a U.S. citizen, of course, he would pay U.S. taxes on all of his income. But under U.K. law, he'd have to pay U.K. taxes only on the 10 percent received there—*as long as* he never brought any of the Bermuda income into the United Kingdom *and* as long as he could demonstrate that he could fund his life-style expenditures from his U.K. income plus any already accumulated assets he could draw down. The U.K. tax authorities were particularly fond of U.S. Treasury bills (T-bills) as such pre-U.K. accumulations for U.S. expatriates. The 10 percent of salary to be received in the United Kingdom, especially after taxes, would fall far short of meeting the costs of living at the level contemplated by this CEO. Establishing a large, credible, U.S.-based fund of T-bills to be gradually sold over the coming several years to supplement his U.K. income was essential to making this compensation structure work according to plan. Meanwhile, the 90 percent Bermuda-based income (no Bermuda tax, no U.K. tax) would be sent directly to the United States, where we would invest it in a broadly diversified portfolio consisting entirely of equities. This investment strategy would use margin to augment its expected long-term results.

A cursory look at this plan suggests that it should not contain both margin and the T-bills. In fact, however, the inefficiency of the T-bill returns in relation to the margin costs (at the time, very close to a wash) was more than offset by the benefit of not paying the U.K./U.S. tax differential on the Bermuda-based compensation (several million dollars) not subject to U.K. tax.

Aside from special cases like this one, margin should generally be used only after the client has devoted himself to an all-equity portfolio.

The Unexpected

What can go wrong in using margin? Plenty. A plan to manage a concentrated stock position through margin over the long term may be theoretically quite sound, but events in the short-term have a nasty habit of interfering.

Perhaps the worst case I've seen of an otherwise well-designed margin plan gone awry involved a client who—in the midst of the long, deep bear market of 2000–2002—owned about $1 million of a stock we'll call XYZ Co., with a total basis of less than $15,000. Not only was he unwilling to pay the tax cost of diversification, he could not be convinced that the stock wasn't on its way to a $2 or $3 million dollar value—and soon. He owned some other diversified assets, but they were mostly in retirement plans and this client was only in his mid-forties. Access to those retirement resources was a long way off and accumulating more diversified assets in these vehicles would be a very slow, gradual process as annual contributions mounted. So, using the XYZ Co. stock as collateral, we took on margin to purchase several hundred thousand dollars of broadly diversified equities, leaving plenty of equity in the account to protect against market declines, especially in XYZ Co. stock—a prospect I feared but the client did not.

Several months into this strategy, the client lost his job. The search for an acceptable new position was to be a long one, but the client would accept only modest scaling back of his comfortable lifestyle, including expenses for three teenage children and the costs of two residences. In a few months, he had exhausted his short-term cash reserves, and he was going to have to sell assets. Urging him to sell XYZ Co. got us nowhere. To make ends meet, we were forced to sell from the diversified portfolio instead. Then the market headed south, and XYZ Co. was especially hard hit. Nearly every morning during the deepest troughs of the bear market, my first activity of the workday was to see how close we were to a margin call. And as the market continued to decline, we had to sell assets from the account to meet living expenses. Conversations with the client were frequent, intense, and often tense. My best efforts during these darkest hours succeeded only in convincing the client to write covered calls on XYZ Co. stock (more on these derivative devices in chapter 15). This produced some meager cash flow, allowing us to avoid further sales of other, diversified assets and to set a target (higher) price at which the client might be convinced to sell at least some of the XYZ Co. stock.

The story has a relatively happy ending. The client found a new job and the market did recover (including quite a bit of the volatile XYZ Co. stock), but the initial problem remains: concentration in one stock aggravated by a margin balance now a good deal larger than initially intended, because the portfolio had to support lifestyle expenditures for the long period between paychecks. A hard lesson to learn. But even coming this close to the edge was not enough to shake this client's confidence in the prospects for his favored stock holding.

Although this client resisted our advice to do the smarter thing—even in the face of an almost daily threat of a margin call—declines in market value are usually a sharp and convincing wake-up call to clients with a concentrated stock position. Not only do they come face-to-face with the risks that concentration presents; the perceived barriers to action are, ironically, often relaxed. Price declines lessen the fear of the capital gains tax burden that often dissuades owners of concentrated stock from selling. Steep price declines can even generate capital losses, as was the case for the new client described in the introduction to this book. The diversified equities bought on margin could readily generate tax losses because they would have been bought before the general price decline. In that case, capital losses would be available to offset any gains still to be taken in the initial concentrated position. ***Figure 12.3***, for example, shows a concentrated position that had a 50 percent gain at the outset. The concentrated position and the margined-diversified position each subsequently lost 10 percent of its value. The amount of net capital gain reduces from 50 percent to 33.33 percent of the value.

Make no mistake; this is not much of a consolation prize in real economic terms. Without leverage, the client could have initially walked away with $92,500 (= $100,000 – [50,000 × .15]). Now, the result is only $75,500 (= $180,000 – 100,000 debt – [30,000 × .15]).

FIGURE 12.3 **Losses Affect Gains**

	Concentrated Position		Margined Position
Value before decline	$100,000		$100,000
After 10% decline	90,000		90,000
Capital gain (loss)	40,000		(10,000)
Net capital gain		**$30,000**	

Source: Kochis Fitz

Still, the reduction in net capital gains can be enough to help clients overcome their loathing of paying taxes on gains and get directly to a diversification solution by simply selling the concentrated asset.

Margin Calls

The point of using margin is not the thrill of dancing as close to the edge of maximum risk and opportunity as possible. Nevertheless, there is quite a bit of room for market performance to be disappointing before a margin call looms. Even if a client uses 100 percent margin (the maximum at the outset) by acquiring diversified assets *equal* to the undiversified collateral, either or both segments of the aggregate can decline substantially before there would be a forced sale to avoid violating the typical 35 percent (maintenance margin) equity requirement. Nevertheless, dealing with margin calls, if they do occur, is no fun. The options for responding to them are few and there's very little time to work within.

Here's how they work: When the amount of funds borrowed increases or the value of the collateral decreases to the maintenance margin limit, the broker announces a margin call. That maintenance margin varies somewhat from broker to broker and from one set of collateral assets to another, but the equity limit required is generally about 35 percent. If that requirement is about to be violated, the broker requires immediate resolution from your client. And if no resolution is forthcoming, the broker can indiscriminately sell any assets in the margin account to restore the required minimum equity. To avoid that, your client will have only hours to achieve remedy. She can add cash or other portfolio assets to the account if she has any available. Often, that's not the case, so something in the account has to be sold. The obvious first choice is the concentrated stock itself, but precisely because values are down, some clients are determined not to sell at this point. The alternative is to sell some of the diversified assets initially purchased with the margin. Doing that will leave the concentrated position intact, but it runs completely counter to the entire purpose of the initial margin strategy. This juncture becomes an excellent, though stressful, time to remind your client of the original plan.

A final alternative is for the client to sell covered call options on the concentrated position, using the proceeds to add to the account to meet the equity requirement. We'll have more to say about covered calls (and other derivative strategies) in chapter 15. It's enough for now to observe that selling covered calls is in itself a low-risk strategy that can be something of an all-purpose cure for the common concentration cold. It provides immediate diversifiable proceeds; prompts sale of the concentrated asset at an even higher, more profitable price; and provides important psychological cover for the client's decision to sell, at least eventually.

Chapter Notes

1. Under the 2003 tax law's 15 percent dividend tax rules, to use 15 percent tax-eligible dividends to offset margin-interest expense, your client must forgo the special 15 percent tax rate. This means that the tax on those dividends is zero because they are offset by the interest expense. If your client has enough *other* investment income to fully absorb the interest expense in the current year or anticipates having that income in some future carryover year, you'd probably want your client to exclude dividends from the current interest-expense allowance calculation.

2. Stocks, Bonds, Bills, and Inflation, 2004 Yearbook, Ibbotson Associates.

13 Managing Concentration Through an Index Proxy

One of the broadest gulfs in all of investment management separates nontaxable or tax-deferred portfolios from those that produce current tax liability for their owners. For almost the entire history of portfolio management, the nontaxable realms—represented by charitable endowments and qualified pension plans, for example—have dominated the development of investment theory and the accumulated algorithms of investment-management practice. For the sake of analytical convenience, early academic analyses routinely ignored the effects of taxes in teasing out theoretical conclusions.

Taxes are indeed inconvenient, but clients aren't permitted to ignore them.

Tax Management

Beginning in the mid-1990s, forward-thinking academics and practical investment managers began to articulate theory to match the longstanding practice of advisers dealing with individual clients who must pay taxes. Under the general heading of "active tax management," tracking each lot purchased according to acquisition date and purchase price permitted sales decisions based both on awareness of the capital gains holding period and the resulting gain or loss measured from that lot's basis. So for portfolios in which taxes matter, otherwise appropriate sales could optimize after-tax results by

- preferring long-term gains to short-term,
- minimizing the amount of taxable gain, or
- harvesting available losses either to offset current or future gains or to offset ordinary income to the extent possible.

These transaction preferences have become embedded in the practices of most wealth managers who serve individuals. Kochis Fitz, for example, tracks every lot in a client's taxable accounts by acquisition cost and purchase date. This record permits us to weigh the relative benefits of accepting a smaller gain that might still be short-term versus a larger gain that's already long-term given the differential in taxes that would result. It also permits us to judge whether the alternative investment would justify accepting a short-term gain when no long-term gains are available in the holding to be sold. For example, if a $100,000 gain in a $500,000 position would become long-term in four months and thus, if postponed, save $20,000 in tax (35 percent short-term federal rate versus the 15 percent long-term rate), the return advantage of the target investment would have to be a whopping 4 percent ($20,000/$500,000) in just that four-month period, or more than a 12 percent annualized return *advantage*.

This growing awareness of tax management coincided with the development of sophisticated analytical tools that used newly available computing power to optimize the selection of securities to closely mimic the performance of equity indexes, using only a small fraction of the total number of stocks in the index: an index proxy. Armed with effective optimization tools and with the practice methodology of tax management, investment managers of taxable portfolios are now able to maintain very close adherence to the results of a target index *and* improve on its after-tax return by optimizing the portfolio's tax consequences. They can minimize realized gains and use harvested losses to offset the gains actually taken. The proceeds of both sets of transactions can then be reinvested in newly selected specific securities to continue to achieve results that closely approximate the target index.

The Index-Proxy Account

We've used index-proxy accounts—primarily as a tax-management technique—extensively for many clients who have large allocations to large-capitalization domestic stocks. As an alternative to either index mutual funds or exchange-traded funds (ETFs), we often use these accounts to match the Standard & Poor's 500 index component of the client's overall asset allocation. The structure of mutual funds and ETFs do not permit the pass-through of tax losses, which are a major element in managing overall tax consequences of a client portfolio. Separately managed index-proxy accounts are designed to facilitate just such a pass-through, which can be deliberately timed for selected securities. We are convinced that these benefits of tax management more than compensate for the higher costs of the fairly frequent transactions and the cost of installing—or subcontracting—the optimization technology necessary to implement the strategy.

Because an adviser can set the parameters of the optimization technology to emphasize or de-emphasize a particular equity exposure—even to the point of excluding certain sectors or specific stocks—this index-proxy strategy can serve a client's desire to develop a particular version of socially responsible investing. Rather than accept the a priori preferences of a specific socially responsible mutual fund, for example, a client can use this technology to develop a customized socially responsible portfolio. Faced with the burden of actually having to make the subtle decisions about which stock or industry categories are to be chosen or excluded, however, many clients abandon the objective. For most clients—even those with avid objectives about achieving particular social results—the simpler solution of just using the proceeds of broad market performance to fund a specific charity, public policy, or public service activities usually wins the day.

Managing Concentration Risk

For concentrated stock portfolios, index-proxy management is especially valuable because the proceeds of diversification sales can be reinvested in the broad market, but with the managed account's parameters set to exclude the stock the client just sold. For a client diversifying away from a concentrated stock position that happens to have a sizable weight in an index, using an index fund or ETF for the proceeds can be seriously counterproductive. At the weight applicable in midyear 2004, for example, selling General Electric and reinvesting the proceeds in an index fund or ETF representing the S&P 500 would have your client buying back nearly 4 percent of what he just sold and incurring a tax liability for the privilege of doing so.

Taking even greater advantage of this customization technique, tax-managed index-proxy accounts can be used to minimize the tax burden of the diversification sale itself. The example of a recently retired CEO of a large U.S. company will illustrate this. When he became a client of ours not long ago, his portfolio contained a holding of $3 million of his company's stock, with a basis of less than $1.5 million. He was fully prepared to at least gradually sell and diversify but wasn't enthusiastic about the prospective tax toll of nearly $400,000 if done all at once. His investment plan called for an overall allocation of $4 million to large-cap domestic stocks, so instead of selling that preexisting $3 million position, we were able to add $1 million of cash and other diversified assets to create an index-proxy account to envelope the retained concentrated position. As tax losses arose in that diversified envelope, we harvested them, permitting us to gradually liquidate the concentrated core position at almost no net tax cost. After only three years, the concentrated position—originally 75 percent of the total account—was down to less than 50 percent, all the while maintaining very close adherence to the performance of the S&P 500.

All other things being equal, the pace of diversification with this technique tends to accelerate over time. As the first sales occur, the nonconcentrated position gets larger, yielding more opportunity for tax losses to be harvested—to permit more tax-sheltered sales—yielding yet larger nonconcentrated positions. Consequently, depending on the tax basis of the concentrated position and general market performance, complete diversification of the position can happen rapidly. Even in extreme cases, the total time required may be no more than seven years.

The third and, in our experience, most common use of tax-managed index-proxy accounts for concentrated stock positions is to manage the risk of concentrated positions that clients must or wish to retain for some number of years. Here, the selection parameters of the account can be set to avoid purchasing any more of the already concentrated stock while still maintaining close adherence to index results by appropriately selecting other securities.

We have this technique in place for a large number of our corporate executive clients who have large exposures to their employers' stock through long shares, restricted stock, options, and other company stock-based assets. The CEO of company X has her account set to avoid acquiring any company X stock; the CFO of company Y has an account that avoids buying Y; and so on.

A great advantage of this technique in terms of the overall portfolio strategy is its dynamism. As diversification sales take place in the concentrated position, the prohibitions in the selection parameters of the tax-managed account can be relaxed, or should company A be acquired for stock in company B, the parameters can be reset to exclude buying B.

Limitations and Drawbacks

Valuable as it is, the tax-managed index-proxy account is not without its handicaps. Here are the key problems to be aware of.

Asset-Class Limitations

In our view, the biggest drawback to the general usefulness of the tax-managed account technique is that it's currently limited to indexes of large U.S. stocks. Even within that realm, moreover, there is little ability to manage toward a targeted exposure to either growth or value stocks. International exposures can be accomplished, at some level, using American depositary receipts (ADRs), but that choice leaves out small-cap overseas stocks and most emerging-market buys. Even within the domestic U.S. market, it is difficult to create an index proxy efficiently for small-company stocks because of their larger bid-asked spreads. Consequently, given the present state of the technological art, tax-managed proxy accounts are not a comprehensive solution. In some important stock asset classes, no current opportunity exists; and in some others, the cost-benefit trade-offs don't justify the investment.

This limitation does not apply, however, to large-cap domestic stocks, the asset class in which many concentration problems are found. Here, the tax-managed index-proxy account serves as a very appropriate tool.

Tracking Error

Tracking error—which is an unavoidable cost of the index-proxy approach—is the failure to meet the exact performance results of the target index. That degree of error can be unacceptably large when the proxy is attempting to match overseas indices or even small-cap indices in the United States. For large-cap indices, the tracking error can be kept quite small, depending on the size of the overall tax-managed account and on the number of stocks permitted to constitute the index proxy. ***Figure 13.1*** presents estimates of the achievable tracking error for two portfolios of different sizes and a range of stocks to be used in approximating the S&P 500 index.[1]

The tracking error depends, of course, on the accuracy of the optimization model a wealth manager uses and can be subject to subtleties like the model's observing the "wash-sale rule," which prohibits for at least thirty days any repurchases of any securities that the model chooses to sell to harvest a capital loss. Making sure that the intended tax loss is realized for current reporting purposes can increase the tracking error. For most people, the benefit of capturing the tax loss far outweighs the cost of the tracking error.

FIGURE 13.1 **Tracking Error**

	Number of Securities		
Portfolio Value	**40**	**120**	**200**
$ 250,000	2.42%	1.19%	1.03%
1,000,000	2.47	1.13	0.96

Source: Kochis Fitz

More important, it's easier for individuals to accept tracking error than it is for institutions. With their closely monitored adherence to fiduciary performance expectations, many institutional portfolio managers see minimizing tracking error as a significant concern. Most individuals are much more concerned with their portfolio's *absolute* performance, especially if they're being counseled to let go of the expectation of getting superior performance from their concentrated stock. Their measuring stick for the alternative is usually not some index but rather the results the concentrated position itself would have achieved. If the diversified proceeds do better, the plan is a success; if not, clients are likely to consider it a failure, no matter how small the index-tracking error may be.

Higher Expenses

One of the great advantages of index mutual funds and ETFs is their very low cost, generally between 5 and 20 basis points per year. To establish a separately managed index-proxy account requires the wealth manager either to install multifactor optimization technology[2] or to engage a subcontractor with such an installation, as well as a track record of successful implementation, to handle the portfolio transaction. The cost of a portfolio-management subcontractor can range from 30 to 100 basis points. Although these incremental burdens on net investment performance can be fairly easy to justify as part of a strategy for managing concentration risk, it's a harder sell when the expected benefits come only from tax management. If the goal were not to manage a concentrated position but only to match an index for a relatively small holding (say less than $500,000) and not be overly exposed to taxes in the process, the appeal of an ETF at less than 10 basis points can be convincing.

Index proxies can also generate greater overall cost because they may generate a significant volume of transactions. Optimization trades may occur at any time, but monthly or quarterly transaction sets are the norm. At those points, however, sales and purchases of many securities are likely, possibly giving rise to substantial brokerage costs. Here is another opportunity to negotiate a low commission rate per transaction, or even a small asset-based fee instead, to compensate the broker while controlling the client's costs.

Deferred Tax Liability

One of the sad outcomes of the aggressive tax management of the index-proxy portfolio is the gradual buildup of unrealized capital gains. Because the client aggressively harvests any losses and avoids realized gains over the years, the portfolio will in time accumulate—your client hopes—a large net gain. In the best of circumstances, a client with a highly tax-exposed *concentrated* position transforms that into a highly tax-exposed but *diversified* portfolio.

This large gain takes approximately five to seven years to accumulate, so lower future tax rates or even a stepped-up basis could ease the ultimate tax burden. As we've seen elsewhere, however, the benefits of stepped-up basis as a solution to the risk problems of a concentrated position are seldom persuasive. Because of a diversified portfolio's reduced investment risk, the benefits of stepped-up basis are somewhat better—but not much more. Ultimately, a tax bill, albeit postponed for perhaps several years, is probably the best tax result your client can hope for in an index proxy account.

NOTWITHSTANDING these constraints, potential advances in theory and technology offer the hope for even greater opportunity to use the intersection of tax-management portfolio techniques and reliable target-performance approximation to manage concentrated stock positions. Additional asset classes could develop robust solutions, and tracking error could diminish further. Greater demand for this strategy will engender additional providers, and the increased competition for investors' assets should reduce costs. In the meantime, the tax-managed index-proxy approach provides an excellent management technique for many concentrated stock positions: reducing investment risk and deferring taxes, with substantial flexibility and complete liquidity along the way.

Chapter Notes

1. Excerpted from research materials presented by Aperio Group LLC, Larkspur, CA, 2003.

2. Barra, Vestek, Wilshire Associates, and Northfield Associates all offer multifactor optimizers that can minimize tracking error for a constrained number of securities.

14 Exchange Funds

The special investment partnerships called exchange funds have been used as a concentration-management technique for many years. The exchange fund was a precursor to the index-proxy account, though certainly a much cruder version (see chapter 13). The core advantage of an exchange fund is made possible by tax law[1] authorizing the transfer of a single, concentrated asset with low income tax basis to a much larger portfolio of diversified assets and deferring any capital gains taxes until those diversified assets are eventually sold. The client's original basis in the stock contributed to the fund is transferred to the client's share of the entire collection of assets in the fund, and the client participates pro rata in the overall results of that entire collection.

Managing the concentration in an exchange fund does *not* involve planned sales of its assets or harvesting losses to offset gains taken on the concentrated position, as is the case with the use of an index-proxy account. Instead, the assets are held rigidly constant until they're distributed pro rata to the fund's investors. Only when those investors sell any of their distributed collection of holdings are capital gains taxes incurred. An index-proxy account is managed to mimic very closely the performance of a selected index (such as the S&P 500 or Russell 2000), but exchange funds have no specific performance target. Whatever the collection of assets produces is what your client will receive—good, fair, or poor as those returns may turn out to be.

By Invitation Only

Exchange funds were designed initially to respond to diversification needs years ago, when the technology to operate a tax-managed index proxy account was not yet developed and capital gains taxes were much more onerous than today. In the mid-1970s, for example, the combination of direct and indirect federal taxes (the alternative minimum tax combined with the deterioration of other tax advantages) on capital gains could add up to 49.125 percent. State taxes further increased that burden.

Still, advanced portfolio-management technology and much-reduced tax rates in the meantime haven't made exchange funds obsolete. They enjoy the benefits of a long history of respectability, and because they're open only to quite large holdings of well-established companies, they bear the cachet of exclusivity—an attraction for some investors. They also produce handsome fees for their sponsors, which is a strong incentive for the exchange fund sellers, even if the buyers now have cheaper, simpler, and often more effective alternatives.

An exchange fund is not an off-the-shelf product; it's an ad hoc arrangement put together by a brokerage firm or an investment bank to fill a need that the promoter believes is opportune at a time when there is a large enough array of distinct concentrated positions to assemble into one fund. This individuality means that a suitable exchange fund may not be available when your client is interested. And the search can go in two directions: you may go looking for an exchange fund that fits your clients' needs; or if the client's position is large enough and if the stock would be an attractive addition to the fund, the fund promoter may come looking for your client.

To recap, the exchange fund's catch-as-catch-can profile presents three major limitations for using one to manage concentration risk. First, the timing may not be right for your client. Second, exchange funds won't work for just any garden-variety stock position; your client has to be invited in. The most likely candidates are those with positions in very large, well-established domestic companies. And third, the promoter is generally not interested in small positions. The ad hoc search for candidates and construction of the pool can involve significant cost in time and effort. The typical minimum investment is $1 million, and exchange fund sponsors are usually looking for a good deal more.

Costs and Benefits

Even if an exchange fund's entry criteria are not barriers for your client, there may be more significant problems with using the exchange-fund technique. Chief among them for most clients is the long period of illiquidity required. To meet tax-law requirements, the exchange fund must last at least seven years. There is usually no formal opportunity for early withdrawal, and there is no established secondary market. Sometimes the managing brokerage or investment-banking firm can facilitate a sale of an investor's interest in the fund to another fund investor or to a third party. But this sale would likely be at some discount to the market value of the underlying stock holdings in the fund, and of course, the client would lose the tax deferral that prompted the initial decision to invest in an exchange fund. Capital gains taxes would be due immediately as a result of the interim sale.

Another big drawback of exchange funds for most clients is the requirement that the fund hold at least 20 percent of its initial asset value in the form of an illiquid investment. Typically, the fund uses a real estate holding to fulfill this 20 percent requirement. Your client may not want to add a large real estate allocation to his existing portfolio—especially one that equals at least 25 percent of the value of the concentrated position to be invested (so that that illiquid position is 20 percent of the whole). This dilution of opportunity can be far more costly than the 15 percent federal capital gains tax, which is the most that would be taken on an outright sale. What may be worse, the real estate used is not likely to be prime quality. Excellent real estate opportunities can be packaged and sold on their own merits. Real estate used to meet a tax requirement for the packaging of some other main event is not likely to be the kind with the very best investment characteristics.

For all their drawbacks, exchange funds don't tend to come cheap. Management fees in the neighborhood of 2 percent are common, although there really isn't much management involved. The initial selection and construction process is admittedly time-consuming, but the whole point thereafter is to leave the portfolio untouched. The sale of any asset within the exchange fund would trigger tax liability for the contributor of that asset.

Exchange funds promise eventual diversification and deferral of tax. But for diversification, the promise can be hollow. Positions invited to the party tend to be holdings only of the stock of very large domestic corporations. Consequently, a client participating in an exchange fund is likely to be denied the key diversification benefits of moving outside the asset class of the concentrated position itself, to mid- and small-cap stocks and overseas holdings instead.

The opportunistic timing of the creation of exchange funds can diminish true diversification even more. These funds are especially likely to be brought to potential investors when a particular market sector has recently enjoyed exceptional growth. Such growth often leads to many newly wealthy investors looking for ways to manage their new problem—far too much of a single holding in proportion to the rest of their portfolio. Exchange funds brought to market in 1999, for example, gathered up large amounts of Cisco, Dell, Sun, Microsoft, and Oracle, making for a rather dubious attempt to minimize the downside risks of market exposure for a closely correlated position. This was especially problematic, since investors in those high-tech–laden exchange funds were then precluded for seven years from taking any other action on stock they contributed.

The Future of Exchange Funds

At this point, you may be wondering if our firm has ever seen an exchange fund we liked. Frankly, not in a very long while. There was a time when this device was the only respectable alternative for the conservative, blue-chip investor. Over the years, better alternatives have developed and are now broadly used for managing the risk of a concentrated asset that a client wants to retain.

Still, on rare occasions, you may have a client who prefers the exclusivity of an exchange fund, despite all its limitations, or one who finds the seven-year lockup helpful for reasons unrelated to investment optimization. A client looking for an excuse to postpone gifts to eager family members, for example, may find an exchange fund creates the perfect cover.

The number of clients facing such circumstances is probably too few to keep exchange funds alive for much longer. If they do survive, we would expect some reduction in the costs of participation as well as innovations in structure. Instead of potentially second-rate real estate serving as the illiquid component, for example, that 20 percent might be an interest in a private-equity fund. Such features might make exchange funds attractive in their own right for clients who can't get access to such investments otherwise. In any event, private equity is much less likely to echo the typical client's existing asset-class exposure. Similarly, the exchange fund could achieve much broader asset-class diversification and the seven years of nonmanagement would be a lot less chancy if the fund package is designed at the outset to include substantial exposures to index holdings, especially indexes of small-cap or overseas stocks.

A further development could be the market's acceptance of a form of risk pooling, or "insurance," bearing a superficial likeness to exchange funds. At least one organization has developed a new form of investment partnership. That partnership invites holders of select concentrated positions to contribute cash equal to a fraction—say, 10 percent—of the select position, pools those cash positions, buys very low-risk investments with the cash, and then after the passage of, say, five years, protects those partnership investors whose initial positions lose value. Contributing investors are free to continue to hold or sell their concentrated positions, but if at the measuring point, the value of the stock has declined, they receive payment from the pool to recoup all or part of the loss, whether they still own the original position or not. If the price of their stock has increased, the investors have achieved their desired result but the original 10 percent "insurance premium" is not recovered.

If the initial selection of stocks is wisely done to achieve appropriate diversification of the risks and the timeframe is long enough, it seems likely that this approach would protect investors against their specific stock's downside risk. Whether it's better than just paying the tax and diversifying the proceeds or using other strategies will depend on how large the premium is for this risk pooling. For example, if your client's investment opportunity cost is 6 percent and the initial premium is 10 percent of the concentrated stock value, the cumulative cost of this strategy over five years would be 13.38 percent of the stock's initial value. If the client is concerned that the stock price is vulnerable to a price decline greater than 13.38 percent over five years, that 10 percent premium is worthwhile; if the decline is less, that premium for this client would be too high.

Chapter Notes

1. Section 721(a) provides for nonrecognition of gain upon contribution to a partnership that is not an "investment company." Regulations under Section 351 (1.357-1(c)) exclude from the definition of an investment company a partnership that meets certain requirements. Perhaps most important among those requirements is that at least 20 percent of the partnership value must be other than stock and securities.

15 Derivatives and Hedges: Buying Time

Derivatives are a common feature of sophisticated portfolio management and frequently used to manage concentrated stock positions of $1 million or more. They are especially popular with advisers who represent the brokerage firms and investment banks that create some of the more elaborate of these devices. Indeed, for some advisers, derivatives are the beginning and the end of the management spectrum for concentrated stock.

Notwithstanding their many dedicated fans, these strategies have a bad reputation among quite a few mainstream advisers, who see them as high risk. Many clients feel the same way. In truth, the risk associated with most commonly used derivative strategies is very low.

Nevertheless, recognize that as your client pursues a derivatives strategy, he enters into what is very likely an unequal relationship. In most cases, the hedge counterparty is likely to be a broadly diversified and reasonably sophisticated investor who's accustomed to transactions of this kind. And, in more customized structures, the counterparty is likely to be a large and sophisticated investment organization that engages in a wide and diversified range of these transactions. It also usually uses some variant of the Black-Scholes option-pricing model to test appropriate pricing among its array of option positions. Chapter 3 criticizes this valuation model when it's misapplied to employee stock options. But the model is well suited here—to short-term market options, the instruments for which it was designed.

To accept the appropriateness of the price, an individual counterparty relies on the efficiency of the options market. In this regard, that individual's position is parallel to that of your client. The position of an institutional counterparty engaged in a custom strategy, however, is not parallel to your client's; it has an advantage: on balance, it expects to profit, having some positions that will win and some that will lose among its diversified positions. Your client, in contrast, is a lone investor, looking to hedge only one position, and has virtually no opportunity to outwit the market in which these option contracts transact.

The Versatile Hedge

Let's review the common hedge strategies, starting with one of the lowest-risk approaches.

Selling Calls

A call option is the right to buy a stock for a period of time at a particular price that is at or higher than the current stock price. For the holder of a concentrated stock position, the attractive choice here is to be a *seller* of a call on some or all of that concentrated stock. The counterparty, the buyer, pays a premium for the right to buy at that fixed price. Advisers and clients should be clear on the understanding that selling calls is generally not about achieving some opportunistic investment advantage; it's about limiting the client's risk.

Call options come in a number of varieties. They're either European or American, uncovered or covered. European options can be transacted only at the end of the term (usually ranging from one month to perhaps two or more years in the future) and are generally used by individual investors only with an over-the-counter, customized collar (as described below). Because European options have less flexible timing, buyers generally pay less to sellers—or strike prices are lower. Otherwise, the standard opportunity is to use American options to reduce the risks of concentrated stock positions.

The owner, that is, the buyer of the option, can transact an American option any time before the option expires. In addition to options that are generally available on the American Stock Exchange or the Chicago Board Options Exchange, concentrated stock owners with large positions can construct *custom* options over the counter. These OTC options give your client considerable flexibility in setting the call price and the maturity date, both of which affect the amount of the premium your client will receive. The lower the call price and the longer the term, the higher the premium the counterparty will be willing to pay.

An investor may sell a call on stock he doesn't actually own. In such a transaction, called an uncovered call, the seller runs the significant risk of having to buy the stock to be sold if the call price is reached—or of having to buy back the call at a price far greater than the premium received on the initial sale. Selling an uncovered call is *not* a low-risk strategy; nor is it a strategy that's helpful to the owner of a concentrated position. Your client already holds the stock. And as long as he can in fact sell it if he has to, selling a covered call on that concentrated position is a very low-risk strategy.

When your client sells a call on a concentrated position, he benefits immediately by receiving the proceeds (call premium) of that sale. He can invest those proceeds in diversified holdings to immediately reduce some of the concentration risk. If the call option eventually expires unexercised, the call premium is taxed as ordinary income. If the call is exercised, the option premium is considered part of the sales price for the stock sale and becomes eligible for capital gains treatment.

Changing a Mindset

Perhaps the greater benefit of selling calls on concentrated stock is that it prepares the client psychologically for the eventual sale of the stock. If your client sells a covered call on the concentrated stock position, the strike price will most likely be higher than the current market price. Selling the stock at that higher price would, of course, produce greater proceeds than the market would offer at the time he sold the call. Consequently, call options are often a convenient way to get clients to commit to a future sale—at a higher price than they could capture today—*and* get paid for the wait. This is not to say they can rely on getting paid enough. Remember, the buyer on the other side of this transaction is probably sophisticated and diversified. Outright sale and diversification of the proceeds *today* could well be the better choice for your client. But capturing the premium on selling a call is better than nothing, and it's often the most effective way to get the client to budge from an initial "no sale, no way" stance.

We've used this approach on several occasions, harnessing the client's enthusiasm about the stock's future price potential to encourage them to capture some of that potential upfront. In one case, the client had already suffered a great deal of loss in her position before engaging our assistance. One of her immutable requirements was that we had to hold on for the price recovery that she was sure would come. We used the fact of a robust market for call options on her stock to confirm that she was not alone in that belief. Three-month options for a strike price $4 over the current value were selling for $1/share. The six-month option, at a strike price of $4 over the current value was selling for $.50/share. And there was still a $.15 premium to be had for the nine-month options. This validation was enough to get her to agree to a plan to sell half of the holding in three equal installments at three, six, and nine months in the future while we bought calls on those share amounts for those maturities and produced cash to put to work elsewhere. Very important, we did not commit to sell only at those higher prices when the sale points arrived. Instead, she agreed to sell those installment amounts at the then market price, even if it never achieved that target value. Moreover, because she still planned to hold on to the other half of the shares no matter what, she was willing to accept that the stock under the calls would be called away from her if the price, in fact, did well. This optimistic perspective on the future price permitted her also to relax her constraint on protection for the downside price possibility. We didn't have to wait for those three-, six-, and nine-month sale points. We could sell that entire half of the shares (and buy back the now-cheaper calls) if the price declined by more than $1 at any point along the way.

In another, not-so-common case, a client who had retired and had already sold his entire position of long shares in the stock of his former employer still held a large number of stock-option grants. They were set to expire in January of each of the next three years, and, consistent with the sequencing logic identified in chapter 3, this client looked to these options for the upside potential the stock might still produce. In the summer before the first of these January expirations, the client wanted to plan for continuing to have the exercise (and the tax) postponed to the following year, but he was becoming concerned that the price might deteriorate in the meantime. The benefit of postponing the tax bill was easy to calculate, and it wasn't much. In taking the current price by exercising now, he had little to lose relative to getting that same price in the following January. But, of course, the client responded, "The price in January could be higher." Ah, yes, the future is never knowable. Rather than be paralyzed by uncertainty, however, a six-month call option on the stock provided an attractive compromise, permitting us to capture *some* value now, softening the blow if the price declined and accelerating some of the winnings if the price did well, while preserving the opportunity to postpone taxes to the following year.

Technically, this was an uncovered call because the client owned no long shares of this stock but only employee stock options. However, the typical risk of the uncovered call didn't actually apply here because he could, at any time before the call option expired, exercise the employer stock options at a fixed price to cover the call option if need be. This client wouldn't mind bringing the tax bill into the current year if he was able to capture that higher stock price.

In selling calls, many clients have had the humbling experience of the stock's market price never getting very close to the strike price (the buyer of the call is the loser in such a case), and they are grateful for having captured at least the call premium. What's more, now chastened, they're more amenable to outright sale of the stock. In other cases, when the option approaches its exercise date, we strongly urge clients to accept the sale of the shares under option. The alternative is to buy the option back—now at a higher price—and thus make a further, potentially substantial investment in a position that's already too large. Almost every client recognizes the scant wisdom of that approach and decides to let the stock be bought away—again, at a higher price and with a call premium already in pocket. There is much consolation.

Buying Puts

Put options are the reverse of call transactions. Here the option holder has the right to sell the stock at a set price within a set time. Your client holding a concentrated stock position is the *buyer* here and pays a premium to the seller of the put for the right to sell the stock at a price that protects the holding from serious declines in market value. The seller, in the meantime, demands the right to short the stock to protect its position, and for that reason, the dividend equivalents on the stock may not qualify for the special 15 percent tax rate available to true dividends. The premium your client pays is a function of the strike price and the option's duration.

This form of insurance can be quite expensive because the premium to be paid could be greater than the amount of potential loss protected. For example, if your client owns stock at $30 per share but wants to purchase a put at, say, $25, the cost could easily be more than $5. The market of course knows that the price can decline below $25 and may demand payment for that risk.

Using a stop-loss order to the client's broker can be a more attractive alternative than a put. The order can last forever (simply instruct the broker to renew it at each expiration) and be much less expensive because there is no charge for having the order in place. Despite these pluses, a stop-loss order is not a perfect choice. The broker is simply directed to sell at the market once the stock reaches that price. There is no guarantee that your client will in fact receive that price if the stock is declining rapidly or "gaps" (never actually trades at the stop loss price, but trades next an an even lower price) perhaps to a much lower price. A put sidesteps these problems because it provides the contractual right to sell at a set price, regardless of what the stock's market price may be at the time.

Still, buying puts also involves the use of resources that fundamentally violate the diversification objective you're advising your client to pursue. The best a put strategy can do is reduce the loss in market value, and your client will have committed otherwise diversifiable funds to buy that protection—an additional investment in an already concentrated position. Of course, all of the upside potential of the stock is retained, but a significant part—perhaps nearly all—of the downside-risk exposure remains. If your client will not or cannot sell the stock position, she will not exercise the put even if the market price declines. Instead, she may be limited to the consolation prize of merely selling the now-more-valuable put. By the way, if your client is an insider, as defined by Rule 16b, put strategies are of no help. Insiders are not permitted to engage in puts on their company stock.

When puts are permitted, they can sometimes help your client obtain liquidity for the concentrated position. With the downside risk limited, lenders may be more willing to extend loan funds and take a pledge of the stock as collateral. The brokerage firm may require a protective put position before it will extend margin credit (see chapter 12). In such cases, however, your client is relinquishing to a third party the right to sell the stock used as collateral—or will be forced to provide even more (otherwise diversifiable) resources to avoid that result—and at an inopportune point, when the concentrated stock's value has declined. This may be a good time to point out to your client that this particular glass is indeed half empty: he would be *paying* for the right to sell later at a *lower price* and *losing tax benefits* on dividends in the meantime. Hmmm. Getting smaller proceeds, incurring opportunity and tax costs, and paying for the privilege of doing so? Why not just sell it—now?

Collars

Not surprisingly, the two option strategies of selling a call or buying a put can be combined to narrow the range of outcomes your client may experience: a reduced downside *and* a limited upside potential for the concentrated position. Selling a call and buying a put to fit the desired range of acceptable outcomes creates a collar for the future price exposure. One can engineer what's called a "cashless collar"—having no net cost to the client—by structuring both options to have the same maturity date and setting the call strike price so

FIGURE 15.1 **Cashless Collar**

	Put	**Call**
Current price	$50	$50
Strike-price range	**45**	**60**
(Cost paid)/premium received	($5)	$5

Source: Kochis Fitz

that its premium equals the cost of the desired downside protection (put strike). For example, if a stock is selling at $50 and the client desires to limit the downside to $45/share for six months, the put price might be $5 per share. To offset that with a $5 call premium, the client would simultaneously sell a six-month call option with a strike price of, say, $60/share. For the next six months, then, the client has narrowed the outcomes to a range of $45–$60/share, at no net cost (see ***Figure 15.1***).

Like any approach using derivatives, a collar is necessarily temporary: options eventually expire. But a cashless collar can be very helpful for managing a concentrated position until a more comprehensive or permanent solution is available. Sometimes a collar is used merely to postpone that solution to a new tax year or until your client can enjoy a lower tax rate. For example, if the concentrated stock appreciated rapidly soon after acquisition, it can be worthwhile for your client to secure at least most of the position's value for a time, until it qualifies for long-term capital gains treatment.

Similarly, protecting the stock's value until an anticipated career event can be another good use for a cashless collar. One of our clients, for example, was anticipating a major promotion within the next several months. Selling the company stock before that event just wouldn't do. Nevertheless, the client was eager to capture the stock's current value and move on to a diversified portfolio, although he feared that the stock price could suffer while he was waiting for this next career plateau, with its attendant salary increase

FIGURE 15.2 **Put-Spread Collar**

	Put		Call
Current price	$50		$50
Strike-price range		45–65	
Retained exposure			
Downside	0–25 and 45–50		
Upside			50–65

Source: Kochis Fitz

and new options grant. Buying a put would limit his downside, but it wasn't going to be cheap. The solution was to pair the put with a call whose premium would cover the cost of buying the put to create a cashless collar.

The Put-Spread Collar

The put-spread collar, a special variation on a collar, permits your client to expand the upside of the range. By accepting a greater degree of the risk of stock prices falling well below the current value, she can raise the collar's call strike price. For example, if in Figure 15.1, your client were also willing to accept all the risk that the stock price will decline below, say, $25 per share, the counterparty's exposure would be limited to only the "put spread": from $45 to $25 per share, not the entire risk down to zero. In exchange, the available call strike price might rise to something like $65 per share instead of only $60 (see ***Figure 15.2***).

Tax Consequences of Derivatives

The tax consequences of derivative transactions depend on what eventually happens and when, as summarized in ***Figure 15.3***.

FIGURE 15.3 **Tax Consequences of Puts/Calls**

	Purchaser of a Put	**Seller of a Call**
Purchase of a put	No immediate tax consequence	N/A
Sale of a call	N/A	No immediate tax consequence
Expires unexercised	Short-term* capital loss	Short-term* capital gain
Sale of the put option before expiration	Capital gain or loss, long or short term, depending on holding period	N/A
Purchase of the call option before expiration	N/A	Short-term* capital loss when the option later expires unexercised
Exercised by option holder	Premium initially paid reduces sale proceeds in computing gain or loss on sale	Premium initially received is added to sales proceeds in computing gain or loss on sale

* IRC Section 1234(b) defines these transactions as short-term, regardless of the actual holding period.

Source: Kochis Fitz

The Forward Contract

Forward contracts—commonly called prepaid forward contracts or variable-delivery forward contracts—are becoming widely used in the management of concentrated positions of $3 million or more. They're an attractive means of reducing risk and providing liquidity for a concentrated position a client is *temporarily* unable to sell.

The fundamental elements of the contract are a loan of cash based on a discount from the current value of the holding and then a sale of shares and repayment of the loan at the end of the contract term. How much of the stock is sold depends on the stock price at the end of the contract term. Forward contracts operate much like collars in that they limit the range of eventual outcomes. The least your client will capture is the amount of the original loan—amounts typically range between 70 and 90 percent of the stock's initial value—but she retains some of the stock's upside potential—usually between 15 and 30 percent. Contract durations usually run between one and three years. During that time, the client retains all the shares and their dividends qualify for the favorable 15 percent tax rate. At the end of the contract term, if the price of the stock is below the hedged value, your client delivers all the shares. If its value is greater, she retains a fraction of the shares and delivers only the balance to repay the counterparty. If the stock price has exceeded the upside limit, the shares retained are limited so that the client retains no more than the originally negotiated upside potential; all the rest goes to the counterparty.

Taxes are reckoned when the contract is terminated. The original "loan" amount is treated as the proceeds for the sale of the number of shares delivered. Nevertheless, although the sale occurs at the *end* of the contract term, the risk of the position shifts at the outset and securities law requires that the contract be publicly reported to the SEC. Consequently, prepaid forward contracts are not a comprehensive solution if the threat of adverse publicity has had a role in constraining diversification. ***Figure 15.4*** illustrates these consequences for an initial position of 100,000 shares worth $5 million ($50/share) with a prepaid forward contract for a 90 percent loan amount ($4.5 million), a hedged value of $50/share, and a retained appreciation limit of 20 percent.

The chief difference between a forward contract and a conventional collar is the immediate liquidity the loan provides and the absence of any loan-service payments during the term of the contract. Another, less-fortunate difference, however, is the lack of any market for the arrangement's components during the

FIGURE 15.4 **Prepaid Forward Contracts: A Range of Outcomes**

Stock Price/Share at End of Contract Term	Shares Delivered to Counter-Party	RETAINED BY CLIENT Shares	Value
$35	100,000	0	0
50 (hedged value)	100,000	0	0
60 (20% upside appreciated limit)	83,333	16,667	$1,000,000*
80	87,500	12,500	1,000,000*

* 20% upside on $5,000,000 initial value.

term. Although it's possible (but probably costly) to renegotiate or unwind the contract with the counterparty during the term, the usual expectation is that the contract terms will eventually be settled only between your client and the original counterparty and only at the contract's expiration.

The large, up-front cash payment is of course available to your client to invest entirely in a diversified portfolio, and that's the big attraction of this approach. Regardless of the stock price at the contract's expiration, however, that initial loan value will be the amount of taxable proceeds. Unless your client is quite confident of having the wherewithal to pay the tax on these proceeds from other resources, a crucial component of the initial investment application should be a very low-risk reserve for the eventual tax liability. The tax postponement of a forward contract is in itself a significant advantage but only if your client is well prepared to cover the tax liability when the time comes.

Initial Proceeds, Taxable at End of Contract Term	Gain (Loss) to Counter-Party
$4,500,000	$(1,000,000)
4,500,000	500,000
4,500,000	500,000
4,500,000	2,500,000

Source: Kochis Fitz

A Competitive Market

Our experience indicates that there is considerable interest among brokerage firms in competing for clients' business in these forward contracts. Before the advent of the Sarbanes-Oxley legislation, it was common for a newly public company's investment bank to offer forward contracts to senior management to permit early liquidity during the typical 180-day lockup period. Now, some legal commentators believe that forward contracts, offered by the IPO investment bank as counterparty, may violate the law's provision prohibiting the company from providing or arranging for favorable loan arrangements for officers or directors. How that issue will be resolved is unclear at this point.

Happily, the client who's an IPO executive is likely to have alternative counterparty firms competing for the business. As in any other transaction, you should be alert to opportunities to achieve better terms for your client—namely, higher loan amounts or larger participation in the stock's upside. Firms active as potential counterparties in this business are usually eager to assist you in understanding the alternatives available to your client and in customizing hedge programs that can best meet your clients' needs.

For those clients who will eventually be willing to sell but are currently constrained, prepaid or variable-delivery forward contracts may be the next best thing to an outright current sale.

16 Powers of Concentration

Some clients are swayed by the axiom that all truly great stock wealth is possible only through concentration. Diversification may make wonderful mathematical sense for other investors, but these clients cherish the possibility of riches—however improbable that outcome may be—even in the face of substantial risk of loss.

This notion is partly a cultural artifact. Optimism and risk taking are deeply ingrained in the American psyche. For all the admiration, envy, or disdain they trigger, spectacularly rich entrepreneurs, founders, and corporate leaders are among the strongest icons in our culture. That there are so few such Olympians is largely ignored. For some clients, then, accepting the risks of concentration is far less about money than it is about self-image, the esteem of others, or even mere fame. And once-successful risk takers are especially difficult to convince that they can't expect to always repeat excellent results. Even those willing to acknowledge an element of luck assume that, of course, they'll be lucky again.

Many may be tempted to dismiss this opportunism, whatever its cause, as foolish, naive, or even venal. It's not that simple. Some opportunistic clients may exhibit one or all of these faults, but others are on the right path—especially those that have gone to the trouble of defining their goals and assessing the risks they can afford to take to reach them.

Embracing Risk

Advisers play a critical role in helping clients answer the threshold question of how much risk they can afford. One of the most fundamental steps of all financial advice is to determine what resources, offering relatively low-risk investment returns, will be needed to meet a client's core financial goals. In one form or another, a capital-needs analysis uncovers the required amounts, earning some base rate of return, that will be required to accomplish a client's objectives over a relevant time frame. The higher the returns assumed, the fewer resources required. But the more ambitious the objectives, the higher the assumed inflation, and the longer the time frame, the more resources required.

Most clients become enthusiastic about this process of evaluating numerous alternative approaches to addressing an unknowable future and, after considering several, arrive at a conclusion about what is a reasonably probable plan for their financial future. The resources necessary to fund that plan prudently cannot be placed at great risk. Clients can, however, put at risk—even potentially great risk—any amounts that exceed what's needed, because doing so does not jeopardize the core objectives. They can afford to lose those surplus resources.

In such cases, clients can go in either of two directions: they can pursue much *less* risk because the total resources are more than enough to achieve their goals, or they can accept *more* risk for that surplus in hopes of more return. When we encounter this decision point with our corporate executive clients who have concentrated employer-stock holdings, they're happy at first to know that they can afford to retain some of their position without adding any exceptional risk to achieve their core objectives. They need diversify only some of the holding, and they can keep the rest.

Following this comforting realization often comes a second thought: "If I can afford to take risk, why should I take it with this holding? Maybe there are other positions, diversified or concentrated, that offer even higher potential returns. As long as I can afford to lose, why not seek truly exceptional returns? If I win, I may move to a wholly new plateau of opportunity, whether for spending, or philanthropy, or business ventures. If I lose, I won't sacrifice anything that's really important to me."

Some clients, of course, can't quite permit themselves that much financial freedom and select instead a middle ground, continuing to accept risk for the excess resources, but doing so simply by keeping the familiar concentrated position they already have or are acquiring. Others avidly pursue the risk of their concentrated position because they believe it can offer truly exceptional financial returns or because it provides other valuable career benefits.

Making a Section 83(b) election for pre-IPO stock grants or options is a great example of exceptional potential returns (see chapter 6). This election would generally be inappropriate when the stock is already publicly available, but in a pre-IPO context, when more of the stock cannot be acquired on the public market, Section 83(b) can provide gargantuan returns. One client received 100,000 shares of restricted stock upon joining a start-up company. The stock was then priced at $.05 per share. At that value, the tax cost of the election was only about $2,000 (100,000 × $.05 × .40), a very affordable bet for most clients. When the company went public about eighteen months later at $12.50 per share, the total value skyrocketed to $1.25 million. And the differential in tax rates from ordinary income to capital gain on that value was more than $250,000, a 12,500 percent return on the $2,000 initial investment. Having achieved this very handsome reward, this particular client sold most of the holding and used the proceeds to complete the funding of his core portfolio. He left the rest of the winnings, now free to be risked, on the table in hopes of further financial rewards—and, perhaps just as important, his retained stock holding permitted him to remain a respected corporate citizen in an organization that was no longer a mere start-up.

Corporate Stock-Holding Requirements

The expectation that an officer or director of a company will hold company stock has always been widely held. Shareholders and investment analysts are eager to know that the company's strategic and managerial ranks have a personal financial stake in the company's success—a stake that links them directly to the shareholders' risks and rewards. The most emphatic expectations—attached to the most immediate rewards or penalties—have usually been on the part of the director's colleagues or the officer's superiors within the organization. The club is exclusive, and there are dues to be paid.

Until about ten years ago, these shareholding expectations for executives were usually quite vague. Increasingly, however, the shareholdings have been framed in terms of specific amounts to be achieved by a set time. Indeed, the holdings are now often specified as *requirements,* enforced by mandated outcomes of option exercises or restricted share lapses, replacing the individual executive's discretion that used to apply in these decisions. A now common example is the requirement that certain officers hold at least 50 percent of any stock acquired through option exercises until their holdings targets have been met. In the aftermath of the notorious corporate executive stock scandals of the early 2000s, companies are generally raising these targets even higher and some are adding a new element—a long, required holding period for newly acquired shares.

The motivation behind these requirements is understandable—the hope that corporate decision makers will have strong incentive to act in the shareholders' behalf—but the strictures have serious drawbacks, still largely uninvestigated. Indeed, they may not achieve their intended goals. What's more, they could cause some very nasty unintended consequences.

The crux of the problem is an imbalance between the risks borne by insiders who are required to hold substantial volumes of stock for perhaps long periods of time and those faced by other current or potential shareholders. Shareholders in the latter group are free of these holding requirements and also free of most of the risk of securities law constraints on purchases or sales, which significantly burden corporate executives and directors. They are free to buy or sell the stock as their whim or wisdom dictates. If shareholders approve of corporate performance, they can buy more; if they're disappointed, they can sell. Not so for most senior corporate executives most of the time.

Although anchoring executives to the fortunes of the company stock can have some laudable results, it can also backfire. With so much of their personal wealth in jeopardy, senior decision makers may be prone to avoid corporate risks, taking an approach that may be too cautious in the short term for the long-term success of the business. The plight of the executive whose substantial wealth is partly restricted is unlikely to elicit tears from many, but society as a whole may pay a heavy price if these requirements foster a timid, caretaker executive class that's afraid to take intelligent risks.

In this context, then, some clients, with genuine regret, have no choice but to accept these expectations as the price of their own career success. Leaving one large, public company for another doesn't solve the problem. Career advancement is likely to have the same price in any firm; the net effect would be merely substituting one concentrated position for another.

Other clients, however, have no regret. They avidly pursue this targeted concentration as the means to other ends. The salary, the bonuses, the generous pensions, the stock and options wealth—albeit risky because of its concentration—and the ability to command substantial business enterprises, along with the prestige and community standing that usually accompany such positions, are powerful incentives indeed. If your client can afford the risk of the associated concentration, pursuing this kind of opportunity can be hugely rewarding.

Stock Options: The Decision to Hold

One of the most effective ways of acquiring and maintaining target stock holdings is through exercising options and retaining the resulting shares. In some companies, options alone, even if unexercised, count toward the shareholding targets. More commonly, however, executives must own the shares. Unless the target holdings bear time limits that require exercising early in the grant period, the optimal time to exercise for this purpose would be just before the option expires, usually ten years from the date of the original grant. This logic of delay also applies for clients who aren't *required* to hold the shares but genuinely believe that the stock presents their best long-term investment opportunity—and who can afford to be wrong.

Waiting until the option period is about to expire strikes many as counterintuitive. "This is such a great opportunity; let's get in on it right away!" Moves prompted by such eagerness, however, will likely cause the holder to miss the benefit of the option's leverage (see chapter 3). If, in fact, the stock presents a superior investment opportunity, or if the option holder is required to eventually own the stock, he should put off the costs (exercise prices and taxes) as long as possible. The rewards will be what they will be; the only thing your client can control is the timing—and thereby the cost—of the acquisition. The longer that cost is delayed, the greater the option's long-term profit potential.

Nevertheless, there can be reasons to exercise early. The Stock Option Strategy diagram (see page 213) identifies in the left column, the logic of several reasons for not waiting. Recall that in chapter 3, we reviewed the right column of this diagram to evaluate exercises that were to be followed by sales of the shares. Here the focus instead is on exercises to be followed by holding the shares. For many of these "don't delay" reasons, an adviser can calculate precise decision points to permit clients to make confident choices about whether to act now or continue to wait. Such calculations can in some cases help clients to dispassionately reevaluate their decision to hold the concentrated stock at all: "Hmmm. The price has to get that high that soon? Maybe this isn't such a wonderful opportunity after all."

The Golden-Parachute Constraint

The anticipation of a change in control of the corporation—through a merger or an acquisition, for example—could constitute a reason to exercise early. Such events often cause the vesting of stock options to accelerate and other financial benefits to become payable to the company's senior executives as parts of golden-parachute payment arrangements.

Tax law denies the employer deductibility for these benefits and imposes an additional 15 percent excise tax on the recipient if the golden-parachute payment is too large. "Too large" is defined by

Internal Revenue Code Section 280G as a payment more than three times the average of the executive's prior five years of total compensation. If it is, the penalty tax is imposed on the amount that exceeds one times the average.

Some companies have especially generous arrangements and will compensate the executive for any exposure to this 15 percent excise tax by "grossing up" the benefit—that is, increasing the aggregate benefit by the amount of the tax due on the whole. If this happens for your lucky client, the total payments made on your client's behalf can be very large, because the gross-up payment is itself taxable. Such an arrangement could cause an exceptionally large adjusted gross income for the year of the transaction, creating a unique opportunity to engage in a correspondingly large charitable contribution for that year. In one situation, a client's total compensation, severance, and other special merger bonuses moved his adjusted gross income, including the employer's gross-up payments, well in excess of $30 million for the year of the transaction. Anticipating this, we helped the client establish a private foundation and funded it with $5 million of his lowest-basis concentrated stock. Without this once-in-a-lifetime financial bonanza, this client would not have made such a handsome gift, and because of that year's AGI, the timing was also right.

If, as is more often the case, the employer does not gross up for the golden-parachute excise tax, an early exercise of a nonqualified option can be very helpful. The exercise would bring additional ordinary income for the year of exercise, thereby increasing the amount on which the three-times-average safe amount is based and thereby reducing the exposure to the excise tax. Given the events anticipated here (a merger or acquisition on the near horizon), your client will see very little risk of missing the maximum profit opportunity. He planned to hold the exercised stock in any event and, especially so now, to reap the premium expected in the merger or acquisition. Incurring the purchase cost a little early pales in comparison to the expected gain.

FIGURE 16.1 **Dividend Required to Justify Early Exercise**

Cost of exercise	
Exercise price	$5.00
Tax on bargain element ($20 × .35)	7.00
	12.00
Annual opportunity cost @ 6% after tax ($12 × .06)	.72
Pretax dividend required to justify early exercise (.72 ÷ .85)	**.85**
Dividend rate required (.85 ÷ 25)	**3.4%**

Source: Kochis Fitz

Capturing Dividends

Under most stock-option plans, unexercised options pay no dividends or equivalents. To receive dividends on the stock, your client must in fact pay the option price (and any tax) to own the stock. It's possible, though rare, for the after-tax dividend received to exceed the after-tax opportunity cost of exercising the option. Advisers can easily calculate what the minimum dividend would have to be to justify an early exercise. Faced with this minimum-dividend threshold, clients almost always back down from an eager, early exercise stance. Adequate payoff is seldom the case. For example, even for a relatively low exercise price of say $5 for a stock selling at $25, if the option is a nonqualified option and your client has a 6 percent after-tax opportunity rate and is in a 35 percent marginal federal tax bracket, the minimum annual dividend to justify an early exercise would need to be $.85 per share, or 3.4 percent of a $25 price, as shown in ***Figure 16.1***.

Change in Tax Rates

Early exercise of nonqualified options can produce a tax-rate advantage, and advisers can calculate the thresholds. Here, the analysis has two subsets. One relates to the client's concern that tax rates on ordinary income may increase (say, from the current federal maximum of 35 percent to something higher). Depending on how long the remaining delay in exercise could be (as long as the time remaining before the option expires), the potential future tax rate would have to be high enough to justify paying the exercise cost and the tax early. That rate would typically have to be substantially higher than current rates. For example, continuing the assumptions of a $5 option on a stock currently selling at $25, a 35 percent tax rate, and an opportunity rate of 6 percent, future ordinary income tax rates would have to top 55 percent in five years and 83 percent in ten. Once clients see how much rates would have to increase, their fears usually abate. I've never had a client decide to exercise early for this reason, but they usually need to see the proof first.

The other tax-rate advantage comes with eligibility for long-term capital gains rates. Exercising early starts the holding period for capital gains treatment and sets the basis at the current price, permitting all future price appreciation to be a capital gain. Advisers can calculate what the future appreciation would have to be to justify the costs of current exercise and the current payment of tax. Here, the results often still surprise clients; the threshold for future prices is high enough that many clients decide to wait and see. Continuing the example above, the price of the stock would have to be greater than $62 (better than a 9.6 percent annual growth rate) by the end of a ten-year exercise period to cause the capital gains benefit to outweigh a ten-year carrying cost.

Frequently, however, the client's confidence in the payoff from capital gains treatment is sufficient to make an early exercise the smart move, as long as she plans to hold the stock for the long term in any event.

Incentive Stock Options and the Alternative Minimum Tax

The initial bargain element of an incentive stock option (ISO) is eligible for a substantial advantage. If certain holding periods are met, that initial bargain element can be treated as long-term capital gain (see chapter 3). The downside, however, is the threat of alternative minimum tax (AMT) on that bargain element. Although the logic of this option strategy generally dictates postponing exercise to just before expiration, that can create an AMT that may be much greater than your client can tolerate, especially if he receives grants of ISOs every year. Since your client believes in, or at least hopes for, substantial price appreciation, eventually he would be exercising ISOs every year as their terms ended, with their large expected accumulated bargain elements. If he continues to hold the stock after those exercises, those bargain elements would eventually qualify for long-term capital gains treatment, so that's not the problem. Rather, the large expected bargain elements encompassing ten years of stock-price growth could cause huge AMT exposures year after year, affording no opportunity to absorb the minimum tax credit.

So even though it appears to make especially good sense to postpone ISO exercises as long as possible, it may be wise for your client to begin to exercise early, particularly if he also has nonqualified stock options (NQSOs). Annually alternating ISO and NQSO exercises provides some opportunity to absorb the minimum tax credit from the ISO year in the NQSO year. Another tactic is to exercise NQSOs in the same year as the ISOs to minimize AMT exposure in that year. These approaches often permit a delay in exercises of both kinds of options until very near their expirations.

Gifts of Options

Delaying the exercise of options often produces the greatest advantage for holding the stock when the client transfers the options to his family at a discount (see chapter 8) or transfers them to a charities, especially a charitable remainder trust or a private foundation, and achieves an upfront tax deduction (see chapter 11).

In these cases, the client's confidence in the long-term merits of the stock can be translated into very substantial benefits for family members or charities by combining two advantages: the investment leverage inherent in options with either the discounted transfer value (gifts to family) or the tax deduction (gifts to charity). For family members or charities that are able and willing to be patient, these gifts can turn into very substantial wealth. But this opportunity comes at considerable concentration risk, of course. A client in this position is likely to be a true believer in the long-term rewards of accepting this risk on behalf of the donees and can often structure the gift to remain in control of the actual exercise decision or may at least be persuasive in influencing it.

Charitable Lead Trust

A charitable lead trust (CLT) can be a useful device when your client wants eventually to pass highly appreciating property to family members or other third-party beneficiaries (see chapter 10). The CLT is especially advantageous when interest rates are low and the required annuity or unitrust amounts are likewise low relative to the returns your client expects the concentrated stock to produce. Low interest rates also produce a low value for the gift-taxable remainder interest, since the value of the intervening charitable lead interest would be high. If your client's hopes for the stock pan out, the eventual net value to those remainder beneficiaries can be quite substantial and carry a very low current transfer tax cost.

Company Stock in IRAs or Qualified Retirement Plans

The choice of employer stock in retirement plans is frequently inadvertent or uninformed, but optimistic employees can use employer stock as a deliberate and often particularly advantageous investment choice. Company stock in retirement plans usually counts toward executives' target stock holdings and enjoys more protection from creditors than assets outside these privileged vehicles.

What's more, under federal tax law, employer stock in qualified plans maintained by the employer also enjoys a unique tax advantage. If the plan balance is distributed as a lump sum and contains employer stock, your client can still transfer the other asset values held in the plan to a rollover IRA and retain the employer stock. The basis in that stock (that is, the amount the plan trustee paid for it) is taxable as ordinary income at the time of distribution, but all the net unrealized appreciation (NUA) in the stock is taxed at long-term capital gains rates and only when the stock is later sold.

Like any other appreciated capital asset, the shares can be given to charity, generating a tax deduction at full value, but with no tax liability on the appreciation. Note, however, that these shares do not qualify for stepped-up basis at your client's death. The NUA value is considered "income in respect of a decedent" (IRD) under IRC Section 691. For this reason, the capital gain tax liability remains even after the client's death, but with the possibility of a partially offsetting income tax deduction under Section 691(c). Consequently, a step-up in basis may be a flimsy rationale for continuing to hold stock in other contexts, and here it doesn't apply at all.

With long-term capital gains rates at only 15 percent, this long-standing tax advantage for NUA is enjoying new popularity, motivating a number of optimistic employees to use qualified plans as yet another way to add to their company stock holdings. Still, this advantage requires the departing employee to forgo the significant advantage of rolling over these values into an IRA. That alternative triggers no current tax; it's deferred until distributions occur, beginning as late as age 70½, and then perhaps only in minimum distribution amounts. For some, age 70½ and beyond is a very long way off. Tax deferral with an IRA rollover can be for a very long time. Your client shouldn't give that up too readily.

However aggressive your client may have been along the way, at the time of a lump-sum payment itself, the question remains whether to capture the appreciation up to that point and roll over the entire plan balance into an IRA or continue to bet on the company stock. The younger your client is, the more advantageous the choice of an IRA rollover. Still, the lower the stock's basis (thus the smaller the current tax bill), and the greater the expected *future* performance, the more attractive retaining the employer stock becomes. Consequently, if your client is relatively old, the stock's (currently taxable) basis is very low, and the stock's future performance is still expected to exceed most investment opportunities, the retention of the stock could well be the optimal strategy. Delete one or two of those factors, however, and the IRA rollover often becomes the better choice.

Here, again, advisers can help clients make the best choice by calculating what's at stake at the relevant decision points. ***Figure 16.2***, for

FIGURE 16.2 **Evaluating Rollover versus Retaining Stock**

	Roll Over to IRA	**Retain Stock**
Current value	$1,000,000	$1,000,000
Tax on basis $500,000 (@ 35%)	N/A	(175,000)
Ten-year opportunity cost on tax (@ 6.5% after tax)	N/A	(153,000)
Growth in value in ten years @ 10%	1,594,000	
@ 8.7%		1,303,000
Tax on distribution of stock value ($2,594,000) @ 35%	(908,000)	
Tax on sale of stock ($2,303,000 – 500,000) @ 15%		(270,000)
Net value in ten years	$1,690,000	$1,705,000

Source: Kochis Fitz

example, illustrates the choice for a retiree at the relatively young age of 60, with $1 million of company stock (with a basis of $500,000) in a qualified plan and an investment opportunity rate of 10 percent pretax (6.5 percent after tax) in the IRA rollover alternative. The ongoing appreciation rate required for the company stock to achieve an equivalent net value in ten years would be just under 8.7 percent.

As we've noted before, the risk of not achieving the 10 percent return in diversified investments in the IRA rollover could be a great deal *less* than the risk of not achieving 8.7 percent on the concentrated stock position. But if your client in this example had confidence in the 8.7 percent and could afford to be wrong, using company stock in retirement plans and continuing to hold that stock after distribution would be a smart move.

The Control Premium

One of the classic rationales for pursuing a concentrated stock position is to achieve or maintain control of a company—a goal common to owners of small, private businesses. In such cases, the motivation usually extends well beyond merely attaining portfolio-like investment returns to gaining the compelling psychological benefits of control and identity. For such clients, an adviser's arguments focused on maximizing risk-adjusted portfolio returns often have no effect. The rewards of control operate on an altogether different plane. In these situations, advisers usually can be of more help to their clients by determining whether the theoretical investment risk of this kind of concentration is, in fact, affordable in light of the client's core spending objectives. If it's not, the client's other objectives provide the discipline needed for diversification that theoretical agreements alone could not supply. But if the risk is affordable, indeed, why not pursue the client's dream?

In some cases, even large public companies may be the control target. A client of ours joined forces with other investors and borrowed additional funds to buy just enough of the trading stock of an ailing public company to achieve control. This client served as chair of the company's newly constituted board, and after eighteen months of cost cutting and strategic refocusing, the company was, as planned, acquired by a much larger one in search of both an attractive addition to its business lines and a new CEO. The client had the qualifications the acquirer was looking for and readily stepped into the CEO role for the acquiring company. At last count, his initial investment of less than $5 million had produced more than $50 million in long-equity values, options spread, and restricted stock in the acquiring company. Not a bad result for less than two years of effort.

This was an exceptionally good example of the proper characteristics of legitimate concentration. The risks were affordable; failure would not have jeopardized the client's crucial core goals. The concentrated holdings were to be temporary, as appropriate, to accomplish the return objective. And, most important for the client,

FIGURE 16.3 **Stock Option Strategy**

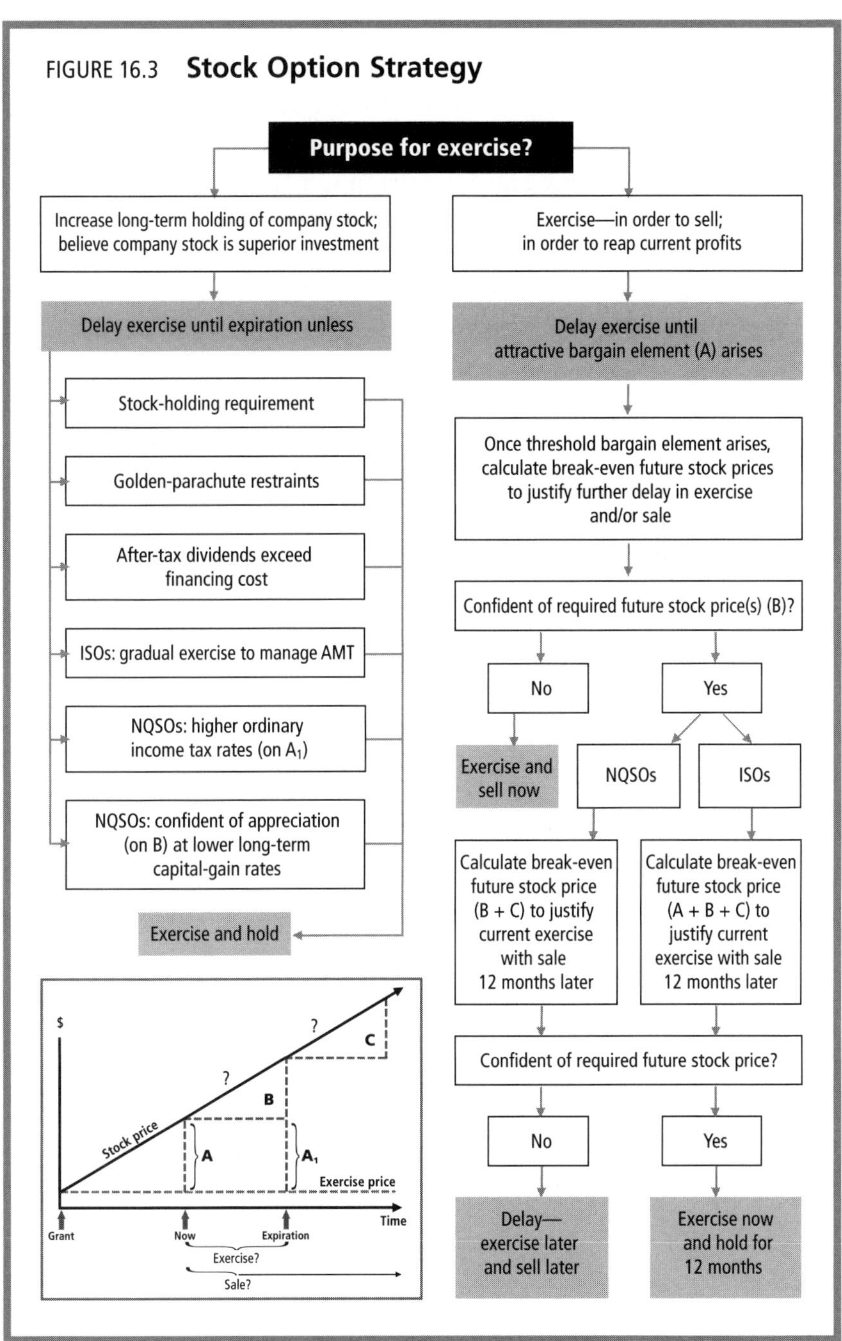

Source: Kochis Fitz © 2004

the potential payoff, in financial and psychological terms, was very large indeed.

Given similar parameters, many clients are prepared to operate beyond the realm of timid calculation and to give boldness the chance to be its own reward. Don't stand in their way.

Afterword

MANAGING THE RISK of concentrated stock in a way that not only makes the most appropriate use of the broad range of techniques available but also responds to a client's individual goals can be a difficult task. Advisers who hope to do this well must develop a better understanding of the many constraints and motivations that cause some clients to resist diversification, even when they know that that's the wisest course. Advisers should also achieve a more tolerant view of some clients' deliberate pursuit of concentration to accomplish their specific goals, a choice that's sometimes very appropriate. These new perspectives are the foundation for this work.

Managing concentration risk can be a multifaceted and highly nuanced response to client concerns. Indeed, it should be. And it can demonstrate an impressive degree of adviser virtuosity, the kind that would be hard to duplicate in other contexts. More important, however, a command of the alternative solutions and the many ways they can be combined can truly optimize the client's financial results.

No concentrated stock position can be managed without first gaining a thorough understanding of what your client really wants to accomplish. Client goals—as illustrated in numerous examples throughout this book—are the fundamental motivators for what the client should do; they also set the boundaries that limit the adviser's field of choices. If they can be achieved at all, these goals are just as crucial to developing the right response to concentration as they are to any other aspect of the client's comprehensive financial plan. Any attempt to solve a concentration problem without developing this understanding is almost certainly going to lack direction and may even backfire.

The well-informed adviser should consider solutions to concentration risks in a particular, logical sequence. That sequence generally proceeds along a continuum of cost, complexity, time commitment, and tax or other regulatory risks. Pursue first the least costly, simplest, and immediate approaches, with the least exposure to tax surprises, before exploring alternatives that are more complex, more expensive to implement, require delays, or run the risk of putting the client at odds with the IRS or other regulators.

Advisers and their clients are faced with what may seem to be an intimidating array of choices, and this book attempts to break them down. The focus goes first to simply selling—or not buying more of—the concentrated stock. This strategy might seem an obvious first choice, but it is often the *last* one clients consider. And many advisers are at least a little disappointed when such simplicity takes the place of more exotic measures. Later chapters deal with the management techniques that solve the problem by giving the stock away, either to loved ones or to charity. In the hands of others, the stock-concentration problem may be defused. Or such recipients may be in a much better position to handle the burdens of sale. The final chapters cover the large variety of techniques for managing the risks of a concentrated position that the client will continue to retain. So, ironically, we end at the point at which so many discussions of concentrated stock begin.

The diagram at right illustrates the full array of responses arranged along this continuum. No single response is going to be right for all clients. Advisers should be very careful to avoid knee-jerk, one-size-fits-all answers. Indeed, it's not even likely that a single approach will be right for any one client.

The real world offers very little that's certain. Investment optimization is always a guessing game about what the future may hold. Some guesses are more logically sound and better informed than others, but perfection is not in the cards. Partial solutions are far better than none. Combinations of solutions are often quite appropriate. This can be true even when a combination for a particular client involves

A Continuum of Concentration Management Strategies

Stock Concentration Management Strategies	Cost/Complexity/Delay/Tax or Regulatory Risks Low ◄──────► High
Sales	Sell long shares; Exercise options/sell shares; Sell under 10b5-1 plans; Coordinate with deferred compensation; Avoid §83b election Low ◄──────► High
Gifts	Outright gifts to family; Gifts in trust to family; Gifts in family limited partnerships; Gifts of stock options to family; Gifts of stock options to charity; Outright gifts to charity; Charitable trusts; Private foundations Low ◄──────► High
Retention	Sell calls; Margined diversification; Buy puts; Prepaid forward contracts; Index proxies; Exchange funds; Collars Low ◄──────► High

Source: Kochis Fitz

both diversification or other ways of limiting risk and a deliberate, opportunistic, unprotected retention strategy within the same total portfolio. But ultimately—especially because there can be no certainty—the simplest, fastest, least costly solutions are very often the best.

Continuing-Education Exam

for CFP Continuing Education Credit
and PACE Recertification Credit

EARN TEN HOURS of credit toward your CFP Board CE requirement as well as PACE Recertification credit by passing the following exam online at www.bloomberg.com/ce, and entering code **77KH33SW**.

All the material has been previewed by the CFP Board of Standards. If you wish to find out if this book and exam can be used to fulfill the CE requirement for a different organization, please contact its governing board directly.

Introduction

1. Which of the following statements about risk tolerance is most accurate?

a. Risk tolerance is a reliable initial input to analysis of client strategies.
b. Risk tolerance should seldom be taken into account; investment returns are more important.
c. Risk tolerance is a derived conclusion of strategies required to meet client objectives.
d. Risk tolerance is unique to each client but never changes for any one client.

Chapter One: Constraints on Managing Concentration Risk

2. Which of the following statements about basis step-up is incorrect?

a. Holding a concentrated stock position in anticipation of basis step-up at death is rarely an optimal strategy.

b. The advantages of basis step-up will improve with scheduled changes in the tax law.
c. Waiting for basis step-up is best for clients who have very low basis, are already elderly, and are unlikely to pursue equity market rates of return for any diversified proceeds while living.
d. The income tax advantages of basis step-up are less than the advantages of avoiding estate tax on the concentrated position.

3. Which of the following is not a requirement of the securities law or the Sarbanes-Oxley Act?

a. Certain holders of stock must report stock transactions to the SEC by the end of the second business day following the transaction.
b. No one can trade on material inside information.
c. A company cannot provide favorable financing for stock purchases for executives that is not available to employees generally.
d. Executives of a newly public company cannot sell stock within a six-month lock-up period.

4. Which of the following is an advantage to the public of stock-based compensation arrangements for corporate executives?

a. Short-term corporate risk taking may be reduced.
b. The interests of executives and shareholders are aligned.
c. Corporate executives can get favorable financing to hold the stock.
d. Executives can be forced to take more risk.

Chapter 2: Sale and Diversification

5. The higher the basis in the concentrated position and the higher the expected return from diversified alternatives, the longer the time required for a sale to break even with keeping the concentrated position.

a. True
b. False

6. Which statement is incorrect? Managing concentration risk by selling shares must take into account

a. the strategy preferences of the adviser

b. the basis in the holding
c. the return potential of the alternative investment
d. gains and losses elsewhere in the portfolio

Chapter 3: Coordinating Long Shares With Stock Options

7. Which of the following statements is correct?

a. The Black-Scholes option-pricing model was designed to value employee stock options.
b. Black-Scholes will calculate the actual cost of stock options.
c. The future value of an option will change over time under the Black-Scholes pricing model.
d. Black-Scholes ignores the specific volatility of a particular stock.

8. Which statement about nonqualified stock options is correct?

a. The bargain element at exercise is subject to ordinary income tax rates but not to FICA or Medicare taxes.
b. The basis in shares acquired includes the amount of the tax payment.
c. The bargain element at exercise is automatically short-term capital gain if the stock is immediately sold.
d. Long-term capital gains rates can apply to the gain that occurs after stock is acquired through exercise of the option.

9. Which statement about incentive stock options is incorrect?

a. Per option grant, no more than $100,000 of the exercise price can vest in any one year.
b. FICA and Medicare taxes apply to the bargain element at exercise.
c. Shares acquired under the option have two different basis amounts, one for regular tax calculations and one for the alternative minimum tax.
d. A client's alternative minimum tax attributable to an ISO exercise in one year is always recovered in some subsequent year.

10. The minimum future prices necessary to justify exercising and holding for one year any single, in-the-money nonqualified stock option will be the same for all in-the-money NQSOs.

a. True
b. False

11. Which statement regarding employee stock-option leverage is correct?

a. Option leverage increases over time.
b. Option leverage declines as the stock price increases.
c. Option leverage requires the optioned stock to outperform alternative investments to achieve equal financial results.
d. Leverage makes options more prone to downside risk for option holders.

12. The best general strategy for reducing concentrated stock risk by selling involves which of the following?

a. Exercising options first and then selling shares from the exercise and any preexisting long shares
b. Selling long shares first and then exercising options and selling the acquired shares
c. Exercising options in January and selling long shares in December
d. Selling long shares in January and exercising options in December

Chapter 4: Diversification Sales and Deferred-Compensation Plans

13. For contemporary deferred-compensation plans, which of the following is the most important feature?

a. Deferring income to lower tax brackets after retirement
b. Protecting the deferred amounts from creditors' claims
c. Minimizing exposure to the alternative minimum tax
d. Providing a tax-deferred investment return

14. For a very senior executive, which of the following is usually the least significant risk of a deferred-compensation plan?

a. The employer's willingness to pay previously deferred amounts
b. The employee's long-term solvency
c. That future ordinary income tax rates will increase enough to outweigh the deferral benefits
d. That inadequate return opportunities are available within the plan

Chapter 5: An Out for Insiders

15. SEC Rule 10b5-1 requires that prearranged sales plans be adopted during quarterly "window periods."

a. True
b. False

16. Which of the following characteristics is not true of a 10b5-1 plan?

a. Suspends the application of the "short-swing" trading rule
b. Provides a defense against claims of trading on inside information
c. Must be adopted when the client has no inside information
d. Can be substituted by giving trading direction to a third party who has no inside information

Chapter 6: Restricted Stock: Tackling Temptation

17. Dividends paid on restricted stock during the restriction period qualify for the maximum 15 percent tax rate on dividends.

a. True
b. False

18. Making an IRC Section 83(b) election may be optimal under which of the following circumstances?

a. The holder's tax bracket will increase by 2 percent by the time restrictions lapse.
b. Additional stock can be purchased on the market.
c. The stock pays a large dividend.
d. There is no publicly available stock.

Chapter 7: Gifts to Family

19. Which of the following is true of intentionally defective grantor trusts?

a. Best used to provide protection of assets from creditor claims
b. Effective means of transferring assets at low transfer tax costs
c. Used to shift income tax liability to the trusts' beneficiaries
d. Used only to transfer concentrated stock positions

20. Lack-of-marketability discounts routinely apply to which of the following?

a. Arrangements under the Uniform Transfers to Minors Act
b. Section 2503(c) trusts
c. Family limited partnerships
d. Outright gifts of concentrated stock

21. Which of the following statements is incorrect?

a. Gift taxes on transfers of concentrated stocks can be reduced by the annual exclusion.
b. Some form of trust or custodial arrangement is a practical necessity for gifts to minors.
c. Each spouse must separately fund any joint gifts.
d. Gift taxes paid can increase the income tax basis of transferred assets.

Chapter 8: Nonqualified Stock Options: Gifts to Family

22. Which of the following statements about transferring employee stock options is incorrect?

a. The transferor of an employee stock option remains liable for the tax liability at exercise of the option.
b. The IRS's position is that the value of the option gift can be calculated only on the date of the transfer.
c. Discounted valuations can be justified by the risk of nonvesting, lack of marketability, and the risk of concentration itself.
d. Incentive stock options cannot be transferred while retaining their incentive characteristics.

23. Which of the following statements is incorrect? Transferring stock options to family members is an excellent estate-planning strategy because of

a. income tax leverage
b. gift tax leverage
c. investment leverage
d. predictably positive investment returns for beneficiaries

Chapter 9: Gifts to Charity

24. A gift of appreciated property can never qualify for the 50 percent of adjusted gross income deduction limitation.

a. True
b. False

25. Which of the following statements is correct? Charitable gifts of appreciated stock are effective concentration-management tools because

a. donors receive a charitable-contribution deduction for the full current value of all donated assets
b. donors can actually achieve a net financial advantage
c. all tax savings from the charitable deduction are achieved in the year of the donation
d. charitable contributions are more expensive in 2005 than they were in 2001

26. Which of the following is not an effective vehicle for transferring concentrated stock to charity?

a. Donor-advised fund
b. Supporting organization
c. Individual retirement account
d. Private foundation

Chapter 10: Charitable Trusts

27. Which of the following statements regarding charitable remainder trusts is correct?

a. The income tax deduction for the donor is deferred until the charity actually receives the trust's value.
b. The capital gains tax liability associated with gifts of concentrated stock positions to such trusts is eliminated.
c. The distribution terms of the trust can be modified as necessary to meet unforeseen circumstances.
d. The payments to noncharitable beneficiaries can be structured to increase over time as the value of the trust increases.

28. Which of the following statements regarding charitable lead trusts is incorrect?

a. These trusts can minimize the gift tax cost of eventually transferring assets to family members.
b. The donor of the trust's assets always pays tax on the trust's earnings.
c. The donation to the trust produces a tax deduction for the donor even when the donor eventually gets the assets back.
d. There is no minimum required payment to charity that the trust must be structured to provide.

Chapter 11: Nonqualified Stock Options: Gifts to Charity

29. Transfer of employee stock options to charity can provide several benefits. Which of the following is not one of them?

a. Larger charitable deductions
b. Improved public image for the exercise transaction
c. Avoidance of tax on the exercise
d. Reduced exposure to securities-law constraints

30. Transfer of employee stock options to charity is best used in which of the following scenarios?

a. The client is optimistic about the stock price and has a strong philanthropic intent.

b. The client is not optimistic about the stock price but has a strong philanthropic intent.
c. The client is optimistic about the stock price but has little interest in charity.
d. The client has no opportunity to use a new additional charitable deduction allowance within the next six years.

Chapter 12: Margin: An Acquired Taste

31. Which of the following statements about margin borrowing is incorrect?

a. The interest rate charged can be inversely related to the size of the margin debt.
b. The size of the margin debt can be more than 50 percent of the value of the account.
c. Dividends in the account qualify for the 15 percent maximum dividend tax rate.
d. Some publicly traded stocks are not marginable.

32. Which of the following is the best statement about a portfolio that comprises a concentrated stock holding used as collateral for margin purchase of additional diversified holdings?

a. Greater liquidity and the expectation of greater net return
b. Reduced risk and greater liquidity
c. Greater net expected return and improved tax status
d. Greater net expected return and reduced risk

Chapter 13: Managing Concentration Through an Index Proxy

33. Which of the following is not an advantage of index proxy accounts?

a. After-tax returns are generally improved by managing the available tax losses.
b. Capital gains tax exposure is deferred indefinitely.
c. Your client can avoid repurchasing part of a concentrated position that has been sold.
d. Your client can create a customized "socially responsible" portfolio.

34. Which of the following statements about portfolio tax management is incorrect?

a. Selling a long-term gain position is always preferable to selling a short-term gain position.
b. Capturing tax losses and observing the "wash-sale rule" can result in increased tracking error.
c. It is necessary to maintain records of the purchase price and date of purchase for each lot purchased.
d. Tax-loss harvesting is worthwhile even if there are no gains to offset.

Chapter 14: Exchange Funds

35. Which of the following is an advantage of exchange funds?

a. Generally low cost
b. Excuse for deferring gift transfer
c. Diversification among asset classes
d. Ready availability

36. Exchange funds must include illiquid assets equal to at least 25 percent of the value of the partnership's collection of concentrated stock assets.

a. True
b. False

Chapter 15: Derivatives and Hedges: Buying Time

37. Which of the following statements about options strategies is incorrect?

a. Selling covered calls on a concentrated position that can be sold is a low-risk strategy.
b. Call premiums must be held in escrow until the option is exercised or expires.
c. A put option is a more reliable technique than a stop-loss order for incurring a particular price for the stock.
d. A "put-spread collar" provides both more upside potential and more downside risk than a conventional collar.

38. Which of the following statements about prepaid forward contracts is correct?

a. Holders of concentrated stock positions retain all of the stock's upside potential.
b. Taxes are deferred until the end of the contract term.
c. The contract itself can be sold at a profit.
d. The transaction requires notification to the SEC only at the end of the contract term.

Chapter 16: Powers of Concentration

39. Reasons to exercise employee stock options before expiration do not include

a. increasing average compensation for IRC Section 280G purposes
b. managing the use of the minimum tax credit for AMT caused by ISOs
c. capturing attractive dividends
d. facilitating the gift of the options to family members

40. Which of the following statements is incorrect?

a. Using IRAs or qualified plans to hold concentrated stock positions is usually unwise if the objective is to diversify.
b. Using IRAs or qualified plans to hold concentrated stock positions provides substantial advantages if the objective is to retain opportunistic concentration.
c. Employer stock distributed from a qualified plan is eligible for eventual basis step-up at the holder's death.
d. Employer stock distributed from a qualified plan is eligible for a charitable-contribution deduction at fair market value.

Index

About Bloomberg

Bloomberg L.P., founded in 1981, is a global information services, news, and media company. Headquartered in New York, the company has sales and news operations worldwide.

Bloomberg, serving customers on six continents, holds a unique position within the financial services industry by providing an unparalleled range of features in a single package known as the BLOOMBERG PROFESSIONAL® service. By addressing the demand for investment performance and efficiency through an exceptional combination of information, analytic, electronic trading, and Straight Through Processing tools, Bloomberg has built a worldwide customer base of corporations, issuers, financial intermediaries, and institutional investors.

BLOOMBERG NEWS®, founded in 1990, provides stories and columns on business, general news, politics, and sports to leading newspapers and magazines throughout the world. BLOOMBERG TELEVISION®, a 24-hour business and financial news network, is produced and distributed globally in seven languages. BLOOMBERG RADIO℠ is an international radio network anchored by flagship station BLOOMBERG® 1130 (WBBR-AM) in New York.

In addition to the BLOOMBERG PRESS® line of books, Bloomberg publishes *BLOOMBERG MARKETS*® and *BLOOMBERG WEALTH MANAGER*® magazines. To learn more about Bloomberg, call a sales representative at:

About the Author

Tim Kochis, CFP, is president of Kochis Fitz Tracy Fitzhugh & Gott, a wealth-management firm with offices in San Francisco and Menlo Park, California. Before forming Kochis Fitz in 1991, he was national director of personal financial planning for Deloitte & Touche and, before that, for Bank of America. Kochis is chair of the Financial Planning Standards Board and former chair of the Foundation for Financial Planning. He has served as president of the CFP Board of Standards and as chair of its board of examiners. He was a cofounder of the U.C. Berkeley Personal Financial Planning program as well as chair of its advisory board and an instructor. Named financial planner of the year in 1987 by the San Francisco chapter of the then International Association of Financial Planning, Kochis has been included in *Worth* magazine's list of the country's best financial advisers each year since the list was first published in 1994. He is a member of the advisory boards of *CCH Financial and Estate Planning,* Kaplan College, and the Capital Trust Company of Delaware. Coauthor with his Kochis Fitz colleagues of *Wealth Management: A Concise Guide to Financial Planning and Investment Management for Wealthy Clients* (CCH, 2003), Kochis is frequently quoted in the *Wall Street Journal, New York Times,* and other publications and is a sought-after speaker for financial and investment forums throughout the world. He earned his MBA from the University of Chicago, his JD from the University of Michigan, and his undergraduate degree from Marquette University. Kochis served in the United States Army, which included a tour of duty in Vietnam, where he received a Purple Heart for wounds received in action. He lives in Oakland and Santa Barbara, California, with his wife, Penelope Wong.

KOCHIS FITZ provides comprehensive financial planning and manages investment portfolios for successful individuals. Most of its clients are senior corporate executives who face the challenges and opportunities that concentrated stock positions present.